REACHING
and
TEACHING
Middle School Learners

We dedicate this book to Penny's children and Susanna's grandchildren
with hopes that their perceptions of school are valued.

Drake Ducharme
Alden Ducharme
Oliver Pflaum
Emma Bonventre
Culver Moskowitz
Dillon Grannis
Hannah Moskowitz

REACHING
and
TEACHING
Middle School Learners

Asking Students to Show Us What Works

PENNY A. BISHOP   SUSANNA W. PFLAUM

CORWIN PRESS
A SAGE Publications Company
Thousand Oaks, California

For information:

Corwin Press
A Sage Publications Company
2455 Teller Road
Thousand Oaks, California 91320
E-mail: order@corwinpress.com

Sage Publications Ltd.
1 Oliver's Yard
55 City Road
London EC1Y 1SP
United Kingdom

Sage Publications India Pvt. Ltd.
B-42, Panchsheel Enclave
Post Box 4109
New Delhi 110 017 India

Printed in the United States of America

Library of Congress Cataloging-in-Publication Data

Bishop, Penny, 1969-
Reaching and teaching middle school learners: asking students to show us what works / Penny A. Bishop, Susanna W. Pflaum.
    p. cm.
Includes bibliographical references and index.
ISBN 1-4129-1478-7 (cloth) — ISBN 1-4129-1479-5 (pbk.)
    1. Middle school teaching—United States. 2. School improvement programs—United States. 3. Teacher-student relationships. I. Pflaum, Susanna W. II. Title.
LB1623.5.B57 2005
373.1102—dc22

2004028751

This book is printed on acid-free paper.

05 06 07 08 09 10 9 8 7 6 5 4 3 2 1

Acquisitions Editor:	Faye Zucker
Editorial Assistant:	Gem Rabanera
Production Editor:	Tracy Alpern
Copy Editor:	Pam Suwinsky
Proofreader:	Andrea Martin
Typesetter:	C&M Digitals (P) Ltd.
Indexer:	Nara Wood
Cover Designer:	Michael Dubowe

Contents

Foreword

During the first two years of my middle school teaching career, I also studied clinical psychology, and it was near the end of that course of study that I took a still memorable course, "Introduction to Projective Testing," a learning experience that fascinates me more than forty years later.

A basic principle in that course was the extent to which people may reveal themselves through their drawings and subsequent related commentary. For example, Buck's *House-Tree-Person* technique invites an individual to draw a house, a tree, and a person on separate sheets of paper. Although the drawn objects are ostensibly just impersonal sketches, the examiner approaches them as self-portraits. A follow-up interview protocol is designed to identify and explore consistencies in the subject's commentary about his or her three drawings. In that course, the clinical applications we observed with adults were fascinating because of the insights skilled examiners drew from this interaction. Although my single semester studying projective testing was rather cursory, I have remained curious and respectful of such efforts to better understand what people think and believe about themselves and their worlds through drawings and related discourse.

As my teaching career continued, I grew increasingly aware of and troubled by the disconnect between the curriculum I was expected to teach, the pedagogy of the day (which differed qualitatively very little if at all from that of high school and college teachers), and the prevailing evaluation and grading utilizing paper and pencil tests. However, the greater my experience, the more I had to confront the reality that so much of what I was doing was only occasionally relevant and useful to my students. I remember struggling with the reality that my efforts were so modestly beneficial to them.

Finally I dared to ask my students to tell me about themselves and their interests, concerns, and questions. I sought their candid feedback about how they learned best and what was least useful in my classes. Thus began a continuing practice of asking students to tell me about themselves, the curriculum they studied that was relevant and useful, the pedagogy that they believed was most effective, and their preferred modes for conveying their learning. After just a few years, my first substantial publication grew from the results of those inquiries, and my career changed profoundly as I discovered there were lots more teachers who shared my anxiety about our work (Stevenson, 1986, 2002).

I think my most revealing and instructive inquiry was a four-year series of interviews with young adolescents around the simple invitation to "tell me about yourself." These 10- to 15-minute interviews were videotaped annually, and once completed it was fascinating to observe a single young person talking about himself or herself at ages 10, 11, 12, and 13, all four vignettes compressed into one hour. Many of the cognitive, social, and physical changes known to occur in these transitional years were documented, but perhaps most intriguing was the extent to which youngsters' core values, expectations, and self-perceptions remained relatively constant. By now a university professor teaching teachers in undergraduate, graduate, and in-service settings, I found this material extremely valuable for grounding developmental theory and research concerning early adolescence.

Although this video interview inquiry was enlightening, it didn't occur to me that it would have been even more useful if I had also invited students to draw themselves and talk about their drawings. However, two savvy educators have seized that opportunity and now share it with you in *Reaching and Teaching Middle School Learners*. Penny Bishop and Susanna Pflaum have wisely and respectfully invited young adolescents to draw in relation to their perceptions of schooling with special emphasis on aspects of teaching they find engaging.

The authors make an important distinction between "engagement" and "pretend-attend"—the behaviors that are often observed in more common time-on-task observations. As part of the research reported here, students talk about their drawings especially in relation to curriculum and pedagogy. The reader will find their insights compelling, guaranteed. It is to be hoped that many others responsible for the growth and nurturance of young adolescents will follow the paths opened up here by Bishop and Pflaum. I have never known an era of educational history more in need of educators to refocus their goals and expectations based on the best knowledge they have and can get about their students. There are oceans of latent knowledge available to teachers who recognize this opportunity and are committed both to informing themselves and then to acting on their best knowledge of their constituents.

The modern middle school movement grew from widespread concern of teachers and others about the same kinds of mismatches between young people and schooling practices that provoked my early restive questions. Now the movement to reform middle level schooling is strongly established through national and state associations, teacher licensure in almost all of the 50 states, an abundance of research and professional publications, and numerous schools where exemplary practice can be observed and studied. In its latest policy declaration, the National Middle School Association goes on public record stating plainly and explicitly, "For schools to be successful, their students must be successful; for students to be successful, the school's organization, curriculum, pedagogy, and programs must be based upon the developmental readiness, needs and interests of young adolescents" (NMSA, 2003, p. 1).

The crucial point is this: it is impossible for anyone to know the readiness, needs, or interests of anyone else without the contribution of a trusting conception by the other person. In brief, if we truly want to know what it is like to be a 12- or 13-year-old, then we must ask the adolescent to tell us. While we can assume in a broad sense some developmental priorities in youngsters' lives, it is impossible to know any student's personal ideas, questions, apprehensions, fears, speculations, and so on without the kind of trustworthy inquirers and deferential context this book describes.

It is vital that not only teachers but also all people involved with middle level education—administrators, parents, community leaders, government bureaucrats—acknowledge this simple truth and commit themselves to drawing from the substantial knowledge that children already have about themselves and each other.

A powerful driving force that overshadows all levels of American education today tragically does not acknowledge this simple truth. The No Child Left Behind Act of 2001 expresses and enforces politically derived demands called "standards" solely through increases in student performance using paper and pencil tests as the tool. The American public is misdirected away from pursuit of the fullest personal and educational potential of youth by a national neurotic obsession with right answers and higher test scores. Judgments about quality have been sacrificed for numbers, an act of naïveté that is to me almost incomprehensible and surely indefensible.

That so many presumably intelligent people can be convinced of the merit of such a limited measure of accomplishment is arguably an indictment of their own education. This diversion away from considering whole children individually in favor of inert scores has nothing to do with youngsters' perceptions except as they perform on such measures. All too often young learners come away from the evaluation experience imposed by NCLB with exaggerated and inaccurate perceptions about their personal strengths or deficiencies. I have interacted with numerous young adolescents who regard themselves as worthless because they did not score high enough. Further, since whole schools are also being evaluated based on their students' test scores, public opinion about school quality and teachers' credibility is also at risk.

The point of view advocated in this book is very much at risk these days, which renders it even more important to all of us. These times beg for perceptive educators who recognize the folly of this national neurosis about testing and who have the courage to explore the far richer and realistic world of possibilities for instructional practices informed by feedback from the learners themselves. Young adolescents generally are mature enough and concerned enough about their well-being to tell us what curriculum and pedagogy work for them, when they are truly learning, and when they believe they are being successful.

All of us who have faith in the potential of students to help us better understand their learning needs and experiences are in debt to Professors Penny Bishop and Susanna Pflaum for their wisdom and guidance as presented in *Reaching and Teaching Middle School Learners*.

Chris Stevenson, PhD
Professor Emeritus
University of Vermont

REFERENCES

National Middle School Association. (2003). *This we believe: Successful schools for young adolescents*. Westerville, OH: Author.

Stevenson, C. (1986). *Teachers as inquirers: Strategies for learning about early adolescents*. Columbus, OH: National Middle School Association.

Stevenson, C. (2002). *Teaching ten to fourteen year olds* (3rd ed.). Boston: Allyn & Bacon.

Preface

One semester when we were both teaching, part time, in the same weekend undergraduate program for adult learners, we started spending Saturday evenings at a pizzeria. Our conversations turned to questions about students' experience of school. In talking, we found we held the common belief that learners possess important, and underrepresented, information about schooling. These conversations led to a research plan, and this book and related work became the fruit of that plan.

This work was in several ways both a continuation of our prior interests and a departure. Penny's main interest is in young adolescents, their needs, and the match of those needs with school. She has been examining middle school structures (Allen-Malley & Bishop, 2000; Bishop & Stevenson, 2000) and seeking understanding of young adolescents' perceptions of school (Boyer & Bishop, 2004) for some time. Literacy and progressive education were in Susanna's background. Some years before these conversations began, Susanna had interviewed college students and their instructor, Dr. Anne Okongwu, at Queens College, CUNY, about the content of a multicultural education course, and although the results were never completed, the different expressions of the "same" experience were uniquely represented by each person. Susanna's work in Africa with Dorian Haarhof, who uses drawing as a method of personal recall, and her efforts in the visual arts as well as prior research experience made the idea of student drawings as research tool attractive. In all of our prior interview studies, we had found that the combination of different modalities provided a fuller, more nuanced view of the phenomena than single reports would have done.

As we talked about ways to capture student experience in detail, we wanted to use interview, but also we felt a need to anchor experience in more than simple recall. We realized that a drawing of a single experience might provide just the anchor we sought. But before we could be certain, we tried out the drawing and interview idea with students of the ages we targeted. And, of course, we investigated prior research that had used drawing as a prime method of exploration. We were captured, and some years later, this work has emerged.

Only after embarking on our quest did we begin to question just what kind of work we were doing. Initially we viewed this as a research project, and in most ways that is what it was. But as we worked with the data the youngsters provided, more and more it was evident that there were strong applications to teachers' practice. It became increasingly apparent that our method could be a powerful form of action research for teachers. Our editor, Faye Zucker, was very helpful in working with us on this question. The result is this, a book about teaching with its base in research.

We write with a hope that several audiences may find this work useful. To turn to you, the reader: If you are a teacher, we offer this book as an example of how classroom practice can be enhanced by inviting students to offer feedback on pedagogy, and on their own learning styles, preferences, and needs. From time to time, we offer reflective questions in boxes throughout the text. We encourage you to pose these questions to yourself, thinking about the learners in your own classroom. If you are studying to become a teacher, think about how what the students present here resonates with your own schooling experience and what you hope to create in a classroom of your own.

If you are an action researcher or are interested in research, we offer the book as an example of classroom-based action research, in which teachers and students can ask important questions and systematically gather data to inform those questions. And if you are a qualitative researcher, we invite you to consider the implications of using participant-produced drawings as a valuable form of visual data to access participant perception.

The book is divided into seven chapters that reflect the themes revealed by students. The first chapter acquaints readers with the context of the study, the importance and complexity of student engagement, the method we used, and two of the students in our study. This chapter is meant to open and explain the whole process of sharing student perceptions of school.

Chapter 2 considers the social underpinnings of student experience. We did not ask the students about their social experiences in school, but few readers will be surprised to learn that the social life of schools is a very important part of these middle school-aged students' perceptions about school experience. We place this discussion early in the book to represent the pervasive impact that social experiences have on learning for young adolescents.

The students we consulted had very strong preferences when it came to pedagogy, and the processes they favor are presented in Chapter 3. Choice, relevance, and action emerge as central to student engagement. Several of these pedagogical themes are echoed in subsequent chapters as well, when we highlight specific content areas.

The first of these chapters, Chapter 4, focuses on how students perceive Math and themselves and on pedagogical approaches the students appreciate. In Chapter 5, the students' perceptions lead us to consider what middle school students need in reading instruction. Chapter 6 returns to issues of inquiry and communication in school experiences of the sciences and social sciences. In particular, a critical thinking approach to current events and writing in the content areas are highlighted as students describe their experiences.

We conclude with Chapter 7, in which we invite our readers to consider creating a classroom in which the learner is regularly consulted and honored as holding important information about schooling. The chapter includes a glimpse into two teachers' classrooms, as they invited their own students to draw and talk about their school experiences. Finally, we suggest ways to adapt the approach of drawing and interview in your own classroom.

We conclude Chapters 2–7 with suggestions about how you might use the ideas in your classrooms. Here we consider the implications of the students' perceptions for classrooms and teachers. We suggest methods that are in alignment with what the students identify as central to engaged learning. We do not want to assert that what is "true" for these middle school students is also "true" for your students. We think of this book as a beginning of a process that we hope you will continue. We hope you will consider how these middle schoolers portrayed their times of learning and use the approach we used in new and creative ways to find how your students experience learning. The journey begins with the material we present here, but it continues as you listen to your learners and adapt practice to deepen their learning engagement.

Acknowledgments

This project has come to fruition in no small part due to the willingness of many people. Because of the need to preserve anonymity, we are unable to name the students who so graciously shared their experiences. The students were quite wonderful, and, though a few complained they were not good artists, most appeared to enjoy the whole process. They were thoughtful and perceptive, and it is from them that we have learned about school learning.

Similarly, we are unable to name the teachers and the principals who so graciously invited us into their schools. The students talked about their school experiences, and the willingness of the teachers to let them do that (and, at times, to do so during valuable class time) is no small thing. We are tremendously grateful to them and to the principals who were so open and helpful. Further, we appreciated the parents' and guardians' willingness to support their children's participation, by providing consent, and, at times, transportation.

Both the University of Vermont and Vermont College of Union Institute and University assisted with helpful research funds.

We are both fortunate to have interested and cooperative family members, many of whom are educators themselves and who were enormously helpful. Susanna extends special thanks to her husband, Joe Grannis. Penny expresses profound appreciation to her husband, Marc Ducharme. Finally, Penny also thanks the members of the Middle Level Teacher Education Program faculty at the University of Vermont, whose outstanding work with students over the past few years provided her the time to focus on this research: Garet Allen-Malley, Kathleen Brinegar, Amy Demarest, Kelly Horgan, Laura Massell, Cynthia Reyes, and Mary Jackman Sullivan, who was an endless source of community-building ideas. We hope this product of such generosity improves learning and teaching for young adolescents.

Penny A. Bishop
Susanna W. Pflaum

Corwin Press acknowledges with gratitude the important contributions of the following manuscript reviewers:

Rita S. King, Educational Consultant, Murfreesboro, Tennessee

Linda Tafel, Professor, Educational Leadership, National-Louis University, Evanston, Illinois

Claudia Mitchell, Faculty of Education, McGill University, Montreal, Quebec

John M. Vitto, School Psychologist and University Instructor, Canfield, Ohio

Notes

An earlier version of Chapter 2 has also been published as Bishop, P., & Pflaum, S. (2005). Middle school students' perceptions of social dimensions as influencers of academic engagement. *Research in Middle Level Education Online, 29*(1).

An earlier version of Chapter 3 has also been published as Bishop, P., & Pflaum, S. (2005). Student perceptions of action, relevance and pace. *Middle School Journal, 36*(4), 4–12.

An earlier version of Chapter 5 has also been published as Pflaum, S., & Bishop, P. (2004). Student perceptions of reading engagement: Learning from the learners. *Journal of Adolescent & Adult Literacy, 48*(3), 202–213.

About the Authors

Penny A. Bishop is Assistant Professor and Director of Middle Level Teacher Education at the University of Vermont, Burlington. She earned a doctorate in Educational Leadership and Policy Studies from the University of Vermont, and her dissertation on middle grades partner teams received the 1998 Distinguished Dissertation Award from the National Association of Secondary School Principals. Before joining the field of teacher education, Penny was a middle school teacher and an assessment consultant for the Vermont Department of Education. She currently consults with teachers and administrators in the areas of school organization, interdisciplinary and partner teaming, and school change. She is the coauthor of *The Power of Two: Partner Teams in Action* and coeditor of *Living and Learning in the Middle Grades: The Dance Continues.* Her articles have appeared in *Middle School Journal, Research in Middle Level Education Online, Current Issues in Middle Level Education,* and *Journal of Adolescent & Adult Literacy.*

Susanna W. Pflaum began teaching in Newton, Massachusetts, in 1959 and has taught Grades 3, 4, and 6 as well as undergraduate- and graduate-level teacher education in various locations. She earned degrees at Radcliffe College (AB), the Harvard Graduate School of Education (MEd), and Florida State University (PhD). She was a professor at the University of Illinois at Chicago; Professor and Dean of the School of Education at Queens College CUNY; Dean of the Graduate School, Bank Street School of Education; Fulbright Professor in Namibia, Africa; and full- and part-time faculty at Vermont College. She authored *The Development of Language and Literacy in Young Children,* edited *Aspects of Reading Education,* and coedited two Corwin books, *Experiencing*

Diversity: Toward Educational Equity and *Celebrating Diverse Voices: Progressive Education and Equity.* She is the author and coauthor of thirty-five articles and chapters. She has led workshops and given many presentations over the past forty-five years. Recently, she cofounded a nonprofit organization that works to support African projects for vulnerable and AIDS-orphaned children, CHABHA: Children Affected by HIV/AIDS.

1

The Case for Consulting Students

Decades of calls for reform have not succeeded in making schools places where all young people want to and are able to learn. It is time to invite students to join the conversations about how we might accomplish that. (Cook-Sather, 2002, p. 9)

What happens when we *do* invite students to join conversations about school and school reform? What are their perspectives, and how might we use those perspectives to shape our practices as educators? This is a book about students' perceptions of academic engagement. In it, we present two central ideas. First, we consider what the fifty-eight middle schoolers in our study identified as central to their learning. Through their words and drawings, we come to see common themes across the group and consider the implications of these needs on classroom practice. Second, and perhaps more important, we urge you as educators to invite your own students into the conversation about schooling, to uncover your own students' perspectives on what engages them in learning. We do not propose that what our middle schoolers convey is what all students experience; rather, this book models an approach to action research that can help you learn from your students and shape life in your classroom based on that new knowledge.

LEARNERS: THE MISSING VOICE IN SCHOOL REFORM

School reform is a centuries-old endeavor. Veteran teachers can attest to the myriad initiatives that spiral through public education in the name of improvement and accountability. Yet, the vast majority of reform efforts rely on adult perspective, on what administrators, legislators, school boards, parents, teachers, and other adult stakeholders identify as central to improving student learning. Rarely are students consulted in attempts at school renewal. In fact, Erickson and Shultz's (1992) speculation on the role of student experience in school improvement more than a decade ago remains relatively true today:

> Virtually no research has been done that places student experience at the center of attention. We do not see student interests and their known and unknown fears. We do not see the mutual influence of students and teachers or see what the student or the teacher thinks or cares about during the course of that mutual influence. If the student is visible at all in a research study he is usually viewed from the perspective of adult educators' interests and ways of seeing. (p. 467)

Soo Hoo (1993) also highlighted the need for student voices in research that inform school change: "Traditionally, students have been overlooked as valuable resources in the restructuring of schools. Few reform efforts have actively sought student participation to inform restructuring efforts" (p. 392). In their discussion of schooling for young adolescents, Dickinson and Erb (1997) underscored this assertion: "Very few of the studies we found were written from teachers' perspectives. None were written from students' points of view. We need more studies written with the voices of teachers and students" (pp. 380–381). And Cook-Sather (2002) openly chided, "There is something fundamentally amiss about building and rebuilding an entire system without consulting at any point those it is ostensibly designed to serve" (p. 3).

We agree. Eliciting students' perspectives on current school initiatives, on instructional practice, and on matters of curriculum can be a powerful and effective means of meeting students' educational needs. Consulting directly the most important stakeholders—the students themselves—is critical to their academic engagement.

ON STUDENT ENGAGEMENT

As we build, and rebuild, the educational system, student achievement remains largely at the center. We know that for students to achieve, they must be engaged (Finn, Pannozzo, & Achilles, 2003). Many factors can increase student engagement, including type of instructional materials (Lee & Anderson, 1993); the subject matter and the authenticity of instructional work (Marks, 2000); and real-world observation, conceptual themes, and self-directed learning (Guthrie & Wigfield, 1997).

But how do we know that students are engaged? Most often, students' academic engagement is measured by adults' observation of students' time on task. Observers determine when and to what extent students are engaged in the learning at hand. Can observers always adequately determine engagement? Surely when writing, planning, or acquiring a new idea, hobby, or skill, we do not always outwardly appear to be attending, even while we are truly "engaged." How often do we appear to be attentive, engrossed in a lecture, a sermon, or even a monologue on the other side of the telephone when in truth we are "miles" away? Young students learn very early to "pretend-attend." They learn to hide their confusion, their sense of failure, their secret off-task fiddling or drawing, their secret communications to friends, all the while giving every indication of attention. Given widespread pretend-attend, how often do we misread a student's level of engagement? And, if we misread engagement, how well can we respond to students' needs? Our method of discovery was to ask students. In the process we learned a lot, not the least of which was that when it is safe to do so, middle grade youngsters really like to talk about their experiences of school.

OUR STUDY AND METHODS

There is a fundamental premise to this book. If we really want to know what engages students, we need to ask them. Schubert and Ayers (1992) wrote, "The secret of teaching is to be found in the local details and the everyday life of teachers. . . . Those who hope to understand teaching must turn at some point to teachers themselves" (p. v). What if one replaced the words *teaching* and *teachers* with *learning* and *learners*? Just as it is important to turn to teachers to understand teaching, we must turn to students to understand learning. Asking students about times when they were actively learning and engaged moves beyond the constraints of observable time on task to uncover the complexities and messiness of true learning.

Learners have much to say about the quality of their schooling experiences. They provide rich insight into what "works" for them and, perhaps even more clearly, what does not. In an attempt to capture these perspectives, we consulted fifty-eight young adolescents in Grades 4 through 8 from six schools, which are described in Table 1.1.

Table 1.1   School and Community Attributes

School	School Type	School Size*	Average Class Size*	% Free/ Reduced Lunch*	Median Income ($)*	Per Pupil Cost ($)*
Town	K–6	300	20	32	40,000	6,000
Village	K–6	100	12	NA	45,000	10,000
Mountain Community	6–8	300	20	26	35,000	6,500
Main Street	K–8	1,000	20	9	70,000	7,500
Crosstown	K–8	275	15	17	46,000	9,500
Southaven	K–6	100	18	39	35,000	7,000

* Approximate numbers to ensure privacy

Stage 1

To understand students' perceptions of engagement, we began by individually interviewing twenty of the students from four of the schools. (Students, teachers, parents, and principals all provided written consent.) We invited students to draw and to talk about their educational experiences. To do this, we used four basic prompts, the exact wording of which varied based on the developmental level of the student:

1. Please describe a typical school day.

2. Please draw a time in school when you were really engaged, focused, and learning a lot, and then describe it.

3. Please draw a time in school when you were not engaged, not focused, and unsuccessful, and then describe it.

4. If you had a magic wand and could change anything about school, what would you change and why?

We asked students to draw in Prompts 2 and 3 because we were mindful of the challenges of reflecting retrospectively on learning tasks. Erickson and Schultz (1992) warned,

> Interviewing after the fact of immediate experience produces retrospective accounts that tend not only to be over rationalized but that, because of the synoptic form, condense the story of engagement in a way that fails to convey the on-line character of the actual engagement. (p. 468)

Drawing provides a powerful window into the minds of children. As a supplement to the interview, drawing placed the students back in the moment, and the feelings surrounding the events emerged. In talking about the pictures, the students elaborated and extended their experiences, and had the opportunity to convey their ideas without relying solely on verbal means. Although educational researchers rarely use drawing to capture what students think about their education (Haney, Russell, & Jackson, 1998; Olson, 1995), drawing can be a powerful lens into learners' perceptions (Haney, Russell, & Bebell, 2004).

We followed these twenty students through to their next school year, visiting them again for a shorter interview. During this second interview, we inquired about various themes that had emerged from the earlier data, including reading and the role of debate and disagreement in students' classrooms. We also had a chance to "member-check," or to ask the students if our interpretations of the previous year's comments and drawings were valid.

Stage 2

Realizing that the power of this approach lay in connecting teachers with their own students' needs, we engaged another thirty-eight young adolescents from the remaining two schools in conversations with their own teachers. We invited two classes to draw and talk about their engagement, and we observed the subsequent learning that ensued as teachers learned about their students' perspectives, triumphs, and challenges. The combination of drawing and talk can be a helpful method for teachers' action research.

At first glance, the students in our study were alike in several ways. They reflected the relative ethnic and racial homogeneity of rural Vermont, for example. And the schools they attended were relatively small when compared to urban standards. Yet, these students were diverse in many important ways as well. We intentionally consulted students who represented a wide range of academic achievement and behavior, socioeconomic status, and grade levels. We invited an even balance of gender. And the students attended schools that employed a wide array of practices, from traditional to more progressive. Their differences are perhaps made most evident, however, when we turn to the students' own words and drawings.

WHAT WE LEARNED

Stacey and Kevin (all names are pseudonyms) were both fourth graders. Both were White and attended small, rural schools. Yet, in many ways they

Figure 1.1 Stacey's Time of Engagement

Figure 1.2 Kevin's Time of Engagement

couldn't have been more different, as they described their schooling experiences.

Stacey eagerly explained, "I like school." When asked to depict a time when she "felt really focused" on what she was learning, Stacey drew her picture (Figure 1.1) and explained, "We're working on a slide show for a biography. And we have a book that we read. And I'm doing Michael

Jordan. And we go on this program called 'PowerPoint.' And it's when you make slides."

Stacey chose to show the colorful laptop computers as a focus in her drawing, with herself as the student seated on the right. She also portrayed the teacher, the larger figure approaching, coming to offer her help. When she and the others have questions, she explained, "We usually ask Mrs. F and she comes over and shows us what to do." Stacey displayed her feeling of connection with her arms reaching to the computer, the desks touching one another, and the availability of the teacher. When asked what she would tell a new student entering her class on the first day, Stacey stated, "That Mrs. F is really nice teacher and you're going to have a lot of fun in our classroom and that we do things different every day." School was such a good match for Stacey, in fact, that she was the one student in our study who could not easily identify a time of disengagement.

Interviewer:	Now I'm going to ask you to do another picture. Only this time it's the opposite. It's a time in school when you're confused or bored or you just don't feel focused. Can you imagine such a time?
Stacey:	No. . . .
I:	Can you ever think of a time when your mind was just wandering?
S:	Not really.
I:	Really? You're always like this, just as focused as this? Never been bored in school?
S:	Not really.
I:	You've never thought, "Oh I wish this class would end."
S:	I like school.

In stark contrast, Kevin's time of engagement was riddled with negativity. Depicting a time when he was writing in his journal (Figure 1.2), he explained that he felt good when he could "accomplish something. And I put journal here because I don't usually accomplish that. And like when I accomplish it and finally get done with it, it feels really good." Even within the act of describing a positive time, Kevin revealed that he did not really enjoy the task of journal writing: "I don't like it because it's boring and because I don't have enough time to think of it."

Although not represented here, Stacey used bright colors in her drawing, symbolic of her feeling of fit; in contrast, Kevin's lack of color symbolized his difficulties. Here there was no helpful teacher approaching him. His hands reaching across significant space for his journal toward the heavily emphasized writing implements suggests how he viewed the task as a stretch. The gap between his needs and his school was well represented by the bars on the door and window in the drawing: school was a metaphorical prison.

How might Kevin's experience become more like Stacey's, in which he felt assistance was always available, in which he felt successful and eager to learn? How might teachers who understand Kevin's perspective close the gap between his needs and his experience? Truly listening to learners opens up a deeper level of understanding between teacher and student.

> How might your teaching change if you asked for students' input?

WHAT YOU CAN LEARN

How might your teaching and classroom change if you asked for students' input? As the examples of Kevin and Stacey illustrated, students can appear outwardly alike and yet have vastly different experiences. We do not propose to offer a recipe—a list of strategies or approaches that work for all students to increase their engagement. On the contrary, the differences among the young adolescents we consulted render such a list impossible. However, we were able to identify some common themes that this group of students found helpful in increasing engagement. We present those themes here to demonstrate how teachers can become reflective practitioners. We encourage you to generate and analyze your own students' drawings and words in order to modify your practice. We hope that by considering this approach to action research, you might invite your own students into the conversation about school and classroom reform.

2 The Social Lives of Schools and Classrooms

[School] gets a chance to be a miniature community, an embryonic society. (Dewey, 1899, p. 41)

Schools are inherently complex social places. Individual students make contact with one another; each observes others and how they communicate; academic successes and failures are played out in public; friendships form and come apart; students learn to share their experiences and to hide their secrets. Regardless of the emphasis on instructional goals and objectives, local and national standards, or matters of curriculum, schools are characterized by the myriad ways in which the students and adults who inhabit them interact with one another.

This is perhaps particularly true of schools that serve young adolescents, for young adolescents often experience intense reactions to social events. The middle school classroom is brimming with dialogue and debate, laughter and tears. It is not surprising that many young students focus more on the personal connections they make each day than they do on the academic events. But what is the relationship between the social climate of the classroom and students' learning? The students in our study felt that a sense of belonging and comfort was critical to their subsequent academic engagement.

In what ways do your students show they want to fit in?

WHAT ADOLESCENT LEARNERS TELL US

These middle schoolers described the critical importance of a sense of belonging and the negatively perceived influences of peer judgment and distraction. Students need to perceive their classrooms as safe spaces, places where they have the authority and support to take personal and intellectual risks, to share their thinking and their work with others. After all, to share their ideas in front of others, especially their peers, requires great courage. And in larger urban schools, where it is less likely that students have known most of their classmates well for many years, trust, privacy, and safety rise even more to the forefront. Not surprisingly, then, as students in our study drew and spoke of their experiences in schools, they helped us understand how very significant their community of peers is in their learning. To illustrate this point, we draw upon the perspectives of four students: Shelley, Laurie, Wildflower, and Ron. The first two highlight the positive influences of community; the latter two depict the negative impact of peer judgment and distraction.

> What do you do in your classroom to help students feel comfortable in the larger group?

Community and Belonging

Shelley: An Eighth Grader

Shelley was an eighth grader who explained through her drawings the important role a sense of community played in her engagement. Shelley's two pictures are thoughtful renditions of the classrooms in which she was learning.

In Figure 2.1, the students are seated in a circle, and a candle in the middle lit the room dimly. In Shelley's words: "We had candles lit and it's something that our teacher says so that nothing that's said in the room would go out of the room and we wouldn't tell anybody and stuff. . . ." The circle of students in Shelley's drawing spilled off the paper, but remained closed.

We look down at the candle, at the circle of students and their writing, and we can see their connectedness to one another. Shelley has represented here the shared focus of the students and the quiet of the room. The use of a candle invited a sense of ritual into the classroom. This sense of community and the group norm, that nothing would leave the room, contributed to Shelley's feeling that it was safe to take risks. This teacher had created a culture of writers in the classroom, and in so doing revealed to Shelley what it felt like to come together as a learning community. This academic experience was intensely social.

Figure 2.1   Shelley's Time of Engagement

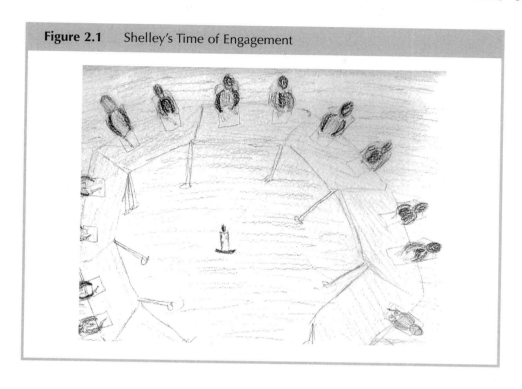

Figure 2.2   Shelley's Time of Disengagement

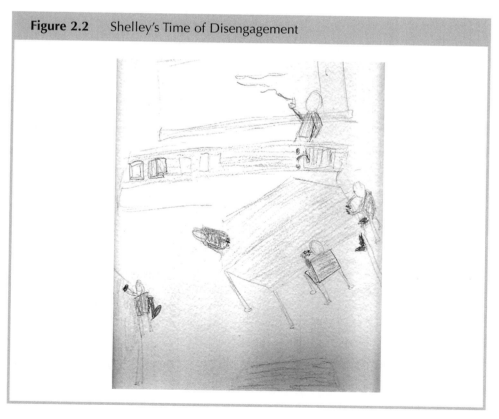

What traditions have you created in your classroom? What is the common purpose?

In Figure 2.2, Shelley drew her Science class. To represent a time when she was not engaged, Shelley depicted the teacher at the board, and herself and her classmates facing in various directions, each separate from the other students.

Shelley explained, "Some people are like fixing their binders and stuff and going through, I don't know, I just noticed one day, I was just looking around at everybody who was looking different ways and doing something and there was like nobody paying attention." She added, "I listen to what she's saying and stuff, but I don't want to just sit there. I don't know. Normally I have something in my hand that I play with." Scattered about Figure 2.2, each student had something different in his or her hand; the circle was broken. No one looked at anyone else, including the teacher, who was depicted as standing with a kind of slouch as she wrote on the board.

Shelley's two very different compositions portrayed two very different experiences. In her "engaged" time, as shown in Figure 2.1, the circle of students and the centered visual focus on the candle symbolized the group norm, the feeling of safety, and the shared purpose. In her "disengaged" time, as shown in Figure 2.2, Shelley demonstrated the complete lack of community during the Science lecture. In the first classroom, there is unity of purpose; in the second, complete disjunction. Boredom and irrelevance produced discomfort, isolation, and the need to distract oneself. For Shelley, clearly, the unity of common purpose in an authentic community is central to engagement.

Laurie: A Seventh Grader

Laurie, a seemingly confident seventh grader, also shed light on the social dimension of schooling. Like Shelley's, her two drawings highlighted vastly different degrees of engagement.

In the first drawing (Figure 2.3), Laurie showed us a group project. She and her classmates constructed a timeline about the Civil War, depicted with group members and with herself at the head. Laurie explained her involvement in the timeline: "Like, me and my friend were like in charge of the whole thing and everybody was involved. . . ." When asked how she and her friend came to be in charge of the project, she replied, "The

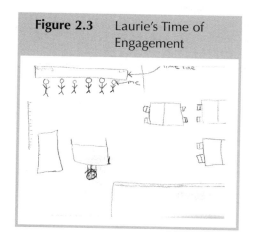

Figure 2.3 Laurie's Time of Engagement

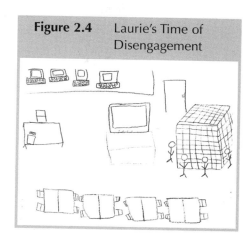

Figure 2.4 Laurie's Time of Disengagement

teacher had to pick a couple people and I like being in charge of stuff, so I always volunteer and . . . just got picked." Although Laurie enjoyed many aspects of the task, such as the hands-on nature and the fact that the end result "looked really good; it was bright and colorful," she explained that this experience was primarily satisfying to her because she played a leadership role. She "got picked," an indicator to her that she belonged and mattered.

Not surprisingly, then, for her second picture (Figure 2.4), Laurie chose to depict a time when she felt socially isolated from a learning opportunity as her example of a detached experience. In the drawing, four figures, involved in their work, surround a huge yellow cube (the large box with a grid on the right). The concept of exclusion, of lack of belonging, came starkly into focus, as Laurie explained that she is not one of the four figures represented.

"We had this project where we had to build a millions cube, well, like, in Math and that's what that is, it is a big millions cube made out of paper and I said, 'OK,' and, like, a lot of people had worked on it and stuff and while other people are out at recess and this is kind of something I didn't do, even though my friends were doing this and it's just kind of weird. They just like—didn't really want others . . . I don't know, it was just kind of weird and so that's something I never really did."

When asked to describe how she felt, Laurie explained that she felt awkward, "not a part of something." In order to portray a lack of engagement, Laurie depicted a time when she felt unwelcome to join a project. Contrasting with the first picture, in which the teacher picked her to lead her classmates, in this instance Laurie would have to insert herself into the activity. Yet, Laurie had a sense that the others did not want her. Just as Shelley moved from an authentic community of learners to a lack of community, Laurie moved from a position of leadership to a position of exclusion. For Laurie, like Shelley, belonging was central to her engagement.

Peer Judgment and Distraction

Wildflower: A Fifth Grader

The relational world of classrooms, when well orchestrated, feels like Shelley's authentic community. The opposite, our student informants taught us, results in a climate wherein it is difficult to engage in learning. Elkind (1984) wrote of the "myth of the imagined audience," in which he described the classic adolescent egocentrism that causes young adolescents to feel as though all eyes are on them. While we would agree with the assertion of this phenomenon as myth, we would add that middle school-aged students are indeed often subjected to the judgment of peers. According to the students in our study, this judgment influenced their ability to engage in the learning at hand.

Wildflower demonstrated this, as she described her conflicting feelings about being in an upcoming Geography contest.

Wildflower described her first drawing (Figure 2.5), explaining that "I felt very excited but I was also very nervous 'cause I wasn't exactly sure I wanted to be in the Geo Bee. . . . I actually got very red in front of my whole class. . . . I was one of the first to be disqualified. I was very . . . nervous and . . . I almost started crying because when I get very nervous I almost always start to cry. And I said to myself, 'You can't cry in front of all these people.'"

Figure 2.5 Wildflower's Time of Engagement

Figure 2.6 Wildflower's Time of Disengagement

Wildflower chose this time to depict an engaged learning experience. She was excited about representing her class in an important event. Yet, it led quickly into concern about how others might perceive her and a pressure to perform without revealing her emotion.

> How can you preserve healthy competition in your classroom, while preserving students' sense of self-worth?

This social importance and self-consciousness was echoed in her illustration of a disengaged experience in school as well. Like her first drawing, Wildflower's second emphasized the dialogue between the players, the essential interaction between people. Here she depicted a time in the third grade, two years earlier, when she learned that her friend Tricia was moving (Figure 2.6). When asked why she chose to draw this moment, she explained, "We were best friends and we were very close and I just didn't understand why she had to move away and she didn't either. She just told me she was moving away and she didn't know why. And her father said that she would understand when she was his age. . . . Her mother and her father were divorced. Her mother lived down in Virginia. And her father had a girl friend that he had just proposed to." When asked how she felt when this happened, she elaborated, "Well I felt . . . I was like sad, and confused, and I just didn't know what to do." With this drawing, Wildflower again returned to her social connections as a central component of school. Less concerned about academics, Wildflower perceived engagement as social interaction.

Ron: A Seventh Grader

The presence of others played a substantial role in Ron's engagement as well. A seventh grader, he chose to show a recent change in the social climate of his classroom through his two depictions.

In his time of disengagement (Figure 2.7), Ron described the challenge inherent on his team as he tried to do his work:

"Everybody had to work on like projects and everybody was like looking over stuff and weren't really like supervised or anything and so like people just started fooling around like sitting under tables, running around and books were like thrown everywhere and paper and chairs were knocked over and it was just like a huge mess."

His drawing of this time is an apt representation of classroom chaos, with the chair on its side, the motion of a student running, and another student sitting on a desk. In it, no teachers are present. He explained that it became so difficult to do his work that he went out into the hall to work

Figure 2.7 Ron's Time of Disengagement

Figure 2.8 Ron's Time of Engagement

on his project, a place where he could focus uninterrupted. Ron's experience emphasizes the role of good classroom management in making active learning work well. In crowded classrooms, it is challenging to establish hands-on projects. Student collaboration will facilitate the process: for example, student groups could decide to take turns in the space needed.

Ron provided his other picture to depict a time of engagement (Figure 2.8). In it, he included a teacher, arms spread wide, and students, seated with a sense of order and focus. Ron eagerly described the teamwide actions taken to improve the classroom climate, this new climate that he illustrates in his drawing.

"Some money got stolen from the play . . . and like a lot of bad things happened so the teachers decided to like go over this, go over like stuff for a few weeks instead of like literature and stuff and . . . that was really like a good learning experience because everybody just like sat down and we did like a project on like how we can improve the environment and stuff like that and everybody was just working and that Mr. S, he just like didn't need to like do anything, he was just walking around and nobody was talking or anything and like fooling around or anything like that. . . . Everybody actually remembered what, like, school was all about. . . ."

> What are the group norms in your classroom?
>
> Who determines them?

With his words and pictures, Ron depicted the shift in climate, from one where students are "fooling around" to one where "everybody actually remembered what, like, school was all about. . . ." Ron became surrounded by a sense of order and focus, where the students, guided by teachers, came together as a community to improve their own environment. A student who enjoys learning, Ron perceived a shift in the communal knowledge of students, that of knowing the purpose of school. With this shift, Ron perceived an important change in his own engagement. Not only was he a member of a community with a common purpose, he was now in an environment that was conducive to learning. While previously the presence of others served as a distraction, he was now able to focus, and he felt empowered by the opportunity to improve their environment.

The students' individual stories were tales of their experiences of belonging and not belonging. These glimpses into the social complexities of school serve as powerful reminders of why we strive to create community in classrooms. These young people depicted and talked about times of self-confidence and of times of felt uncertainty. Laurie's feeling "awkward" and "not a part of something" and Wildflower's self-admonition not to "cry in front of all these people" sit in weighty juxtaposition to the candle in the center of Shelley's poetry circle. Shelley and her peers remind us that the conditions through which we create such community must be authentic.

WHAT THE RESEARCH LITERATURE TELLS US

Middle School Students Require
Teachers Specially Prepared for the Age Group

How educators view the purposes of school undoubtedly affects how students respond. Middle schools, or "junior high schools," have been viewed at times as a required tour of duty by some teachers, who prefer to focus on the curricular matters at hand rather than the distinct needs of the age group. Often, teachers are said to be putting in their time, awaiting the retirement of a senior high faculty member in hopes of moving out of the "trenches" and into the more elite status of high school. In stark contrast, the National Middle School Association (NMSA) and affiliate organizations have worked over the past few decades to radically transform junior versions of high schools into developmentally responsive communities of learning, creating schools staffed by teachers who choose to work at the middle level (Jackson & Davis, 2000; National Middle School Association [NMSA], 1995, 2003).

As children mature earlier and negotiate increasingly complex lives, these teachers who are drawn to the special interests and concerns of young adolescents include their social needs in their pedagogy. They create spaces within classrooms to recognize and celebrate commonalities, study and embrace differences, and examine and generate radical ideas. Children, especially middle schoolers, want to talk with one another, and effective teachers of young adolescents draw on student interests to foster learning (Stevenson, 2002). And their social experiences are a central interest.

Group Affiliation, Belonging, and School Success

Noddings (1992) writes, "Relation, except in very rare cases, precedes any engagement with subject matter" (p. 36). This attention to relation is at the heart of creating classroom spaces where students feel the sense of belonging and affiliation that our young learner Shelley represented in her first picture. Maslow (1954), in his influential work in the area of motivation theory, wrote of belonging or group affiliation as one of the central love or social needs. Glasser (1986), too, identified belonging as critical to the fulfillment of a "quality world." Students need warm, supportive human relationships for school success, as they strive to satisfy four basic psychological needs: belonging, power, freedom, and fun, none of which was present in Shelley's second picture. Many schools have adopted Glasser's control theory, or similar approaches, as the basis for generating a safe and respectful school climate (Martin, 1988). Other schools embrace a traditional Native American child-rearing philosophy, which offers the Circle of Courage, clearly identifying belonging as one of four central needs. This has served as the means for many schools' attempts to enhance student self-concept (Farner, 1996; Passaro et al., 1994).

While a sense of belonging is generally accepted as a social need of humans, there has been particular emphasis placed on this need in early adolescence. The complexity of social development in early adolescence is well documented (for example, Van Hoose, Strahan, & L'Esperance, 2001). We know that affirmations from others, especially from peers, can powerfully impact the young adolescent's self-concept (Beane & Lipka, 1980). The relational context of schools, comprised of the essential interdependence and social nature of people within educational institutions, is rich and complex.

Group Affiliation, Belonging, and At-Risk Behaviors

Belonging appears also to play a critical role in the lives of youth considered to be "at risk" of school failure, with significant relationships being found between student sense of belonging and grade point average (Clasen, 1987). Further, there are strong links between feelings of attachment and belonging with prevention of youth at risk from engaging in criminal behavior (Van Bockern, 1998). Youth gang membership fosters a sense of belonging, and such attending to this need can be useful as a prevention and intervention strategy (Reep, 1996). Among at-risk students, conventional classroom practices fail to engender a sense of belonging (Beck & Malley, 1998). The call for schools to attend to students' needs for affiliation is critically important.

TRANSLATING THEORY INTO PRACTICE

It is the attention to caring relations of which Noddings (1992) writes, and the essential human need for belonging asserted by Maslow (1954), Glasser (1986), and others, that drive many instructional approaches, curricula, and even organizational frameworks in today's schools. The field of early childhood education has long been attentive to the social domain of development (McLean & Mayer, 1996), advocating for practices that respond to the developmental readiness of a child. Middle level education has also been particularly attentive to this call. Many involved in the education of young adolescents challenge schools to be responsive to the social needs of children. Stevenson (2002) asserts, "Meeting these personal human needs must be a primary goal of middle level schooling" (p. 128). We discuss briefly those school features that address young adolescents' need to belong and be known.

Size Matters

It has become increasingly clear that the size of an educational institution has a clear impact on student experience. Small schools, in particular those with enrollments of 350 or fewer, are characterized by more trusting environments (Bryk & Schneider, 2002) and offer a strong sense of community and openness toward change (Wasley, 2000). Research also suggests that school size influences student achievement. This relationship is mediated by the effects on teachers; teachers from smaller schools have demonstrated more positive attitudes, and students have earned higher achievement scores than their counterparts in larger settings (Lee & Loeb, 2000; Lee & Smith, 1993). As a means to capitalize on the positive effects of smaller schools, a school-within-a-school approach has been embraced recently by secondary schools (Schoenlein, 2001; Wasley & Lear, 2001), particularly as schools struggle with the reality of increasing school violence. Many urban schools have created academies or schools-within-schools to foster a smaller school environment that can provide opportunities for students to become known.

In what ways has your school created small communities of learning? What might you try in your own classroom?

Supportive Teams Promote Community

As a means for creating smaller schools, organizations such as the Carnegie Corporation (1995), the Carnegie Council on Adolescent Development (1989), and the National Middle School Association (NMSA) (1995, 2003) have routinely emphasized the importance of creating small communities of learning by promoting the creation of teams. "Creating smaller schools is an important strategy for fostering supportive relationships between teachers and students. In large schools or small, however, creating teams of teachers and students is a vital part of developing a middle grades learning community" (Jackson & Davis, 2000, p. 125). Student sense of belonging is such an overt goal of the teaming initiative, in fact, that it has been used as one criterion against which "highly effective" interdisciplinary teams are sometimes measured (George & Stevenson, 1988).

Interdisciplinary teaming has indeed proven to be a powerful mechanism for enhancing social bonding for at-risk middle level students, in particular (Arhar & Kromrey, 1995). Studies have demonstrated higher student sense of belonging (Arhar, 1994; Wehlage, Rutter, Smith, Lesko, & Fernandez, 1989) and increased interracial cooperation (Metz, 1986) among students on teams.

Teacher Advisories Link All Learners to Supportive Adults

In addition to the organizational structures in schools, such as teaming, many schools respond to their students' need to belong by ensuring that all students be known well by at least one adult in the building. Here is where school and classroom size interact with school organization.

Thus far, the means toward accomplishing this end in most middle schools has been the development of teacher advisories (Carnegie Corporation, 1995; Carnegie Council on Adolescent Development, 1989; NMSA, 1995, 2003). In a teacher advisory system, one adult meets with twelve to fifteen students on a daily basis, for 10 to 30 minutes. In reality, of course, this practice varies widely, based on building-level support, teacher commitment, and numbers of teachers and students. The time is intended to be spent connecting socially and academically, and enables the adult to serve in an advocate role for those students. According to Maerhoff (1990), "Being part of a small advisory group that meets twice a day helps all children—even the socially inept—gain a sense of belonging" (p. 507).

Ideally, the advisory ensures that no child slips through the cracks of public education; ideally, it enables educators to notice, to address issues so that each student's fit with school is enhanced. In actual practice, as our study demonstrated, adolescent learners are likely to continue experiencing social discomfort even when school staff work with them in small teams. The difficulties encountered by middle school students in larger schools, particularly urban schools with high turnover among staff, are often more serious still.

CURRICULUM AND INSTRUCTION THAT PROMOTE BELONGING

A number of curricular approaches also purport to foster a sense of belonging on the part of students.

Service Learning

Service learning, for example, has emerged as distinct from community service, grounded in clear and intentional links to curriculum and offering opportunities for student reflection (Andrus, 1996; Schine, 1997). When students are engaged in service in situations with real learning, the impact on them and others is significant (Conrad & Hedin, 1991). Notable differences in students' sense of belonging to school and community have been found between high school students who participate in service learning and those who do not (Perry, 1998).

In a family literacy project one of us codirected in New York City, we developed an English course entitled "Children's Literature," specifically for teenage mothers. In this course, the young mothers visited nearby elementary schools and read to primary grade students. This experience deepened mothers' understanding of literature, of development, and, most important, of their own self-worth (Johnson, Pflaum, Sherman, Taylor, & Poole, 1996). In projects such as these, where students are engaged in both service and reflection on the service, students come to feel a sense of belonging to a larger community.

Complex Instruction and Equity Pedagogies

Further, complex instruction, a form of cooperative grouping considered as an "equity pedagogy," is also a school response to ensuring that all students belong. When incorporating complex instruction as a strategy, teachers work to create equal-status interaction within small groups, as students use each other as resources to complete challenging group tasks (Cohen & Lotan, 1997).

What different types of "status" are portrayed by students in your classroom?

Responsive Classrooms and Morning Meeting

Schools have responded in varying degrees to the need for students to affiliate themselves with others, to be a part of "something good," as Stevenson (2002, p. 86) writes. Many schools subscribe to intentional approaches toward this end. Three of the four schools in our study, for example, embraced the Responsive Classroom approach (Charney, 1992; Wood, 1999) as a means to create such a culture in their buildings and classrooms. Originating in the elementary grades, the Responsive Classroom approach has been adapted for middle schools as well.

> A teacher using The Responsive Classroom approach makes the social context of teaching and learning a part of her lesson plans each day. Teachers report that it creates the kind of trustworthy space in the classroom where every child's voice becomes important, where learning carries meaning for each child. (Wood, 1999, pp. 225–226)

Two of the schools were divided into interdisciplinary teams, in an attempt to create small communities of learning within the larger school population. In the one school not using the Responsive Classroom approach, the team had created its own teamwide meeting time, held in an amphitheater-style space, in an explicit attempt to build community and identity within the team.

Even when subscribing to specific approaches, however, teachers face challenges with implementation. Wildflower shared her concern about the whole event, as she described the difficulty she experienced during Morning Meeting:

"Sometimes they are just talking with each other about this, about um, the most popular girl in the school and they are not even listening to me and that makes me think like, 'Do they even care? They don't even care, so why do I even share?' Because usually the only one who is listening to me when I do share something is the teacher."

Wildflower's belief that the teacher is "the only one who is listening" to her is the antithesis of the community building the Responsive Classroom advocates. Far from the "trustworthy space" Wood (1999) described, for Wildflower, the Morning Meeting was a time when the social aspect of school confined her voice and undermined her self-confidence. Wildflower's question, "Do they even care?" is an important one, and reminds us that building community in our classrooms requires constant diligence, active listening, and ongoing modeling of positive social behaviors. As we work to build community and to encourage positive social support to learning, we face a challenge in knowing what students are thinking. Children learn early to hide their disappointments, their confusions, their difficulties. In order to help students like Wildflower, we need to imagine how students might respond to her talk at Morning Meeting and help her and others to understand how to interact in positive and authentic ways.

Students and schools alike seemed to acknowledge the need for community and belonging. Yet, even in the best of middle level classroom cultures, the press of conformity is strong. And in classrooms, there is apprehension about the ever-present audience. These are challenges for educators and students alike, challenges that beg for our consideration if we are to enrich and improve students' sense of fit with school.

Young adolescents report "being picked on" as the number one cause of violence in schools (Thornton, 2002). Establishing a community in which students feel a sense of affiliation and belonging is therefore a matter of not only intellectual safety but physical safety as well. Moreover, we assert, the purposes for community activities must be made overt and explicit. Students must feel they are safe in every sense of the word. When schools adopt programs to increase community, the reasons need to be explicit and overt to the learners.

STRATEGIES TO TRY IN YOUR CLASSROOM

The students in our study had strong feelings about the importance of the classroom climate created by teachers. For many students, feeling a sense of belonging is an essential precursor to their academic engagement. What does this mean for teachers, classrooms, teams, and schools? How can we attend to classroom climate? We include here some general suggestions, based on the lessons these middle schoolers taught us.

Create a Personal Community

Personal communities are built through relationships and through explicit talk. Students' relationships with teachers are important. Most middle school students want to know their teachers as whole people. Surely many of us recall the shock and exuberance of running into our grade school teachers at the grocery store for the first time. Teachers who create a personal community in the classroom enter the school each day as whole people—people who share brief anecdotes about life, family, and circumstance. Students come to know what their teachers are passionate about, and what hobbies or interests they possess. As Palmer (1998) states, "Teaching always takes place at the crossroads of the personal and the public, and if I want to teach well, I must learn to stand where these opposites intersect" (p. 63).

Similarly, students need to know one another. Whether teaching at small or large schools, teachers can always find opportunities to build bridges and forge connections between students. Time spent building in "ice breakers" or team-building activities, particularly at the start of the school year or when a new member joins the class, pays off in the long run. Opportunities to laugh together, as well as respond to challenges together, tighten the human bonds of the learning community.

A Few Community-Building Activities

Each of these activities enables students to explore what they have in common with peers as well as what makes them unique. Some are kinesthetic and helpful in getting students moving; others are well suited for quieter, seated conversation.

"Four Corners" Ask students to divide into the four corners of the room, based on birth order (first born, last born, middle child, and single child). Give them 5 minutes to plan as a group how they will convince the other groups that their place in the birth order is best.

"Perfect Saturday" Ask each student to write on an index card how he or she would spend a "perfect Saturday." Collect responses and read aloud, inviting classmates to guess whose perfect day you are reading.

"Two Truths and a Fib" Each student discloses three facts about himself or herself. Two are true, and one is a fib. Peers then guess which item is untrue.

"Uncommon Commonalities" Group students in pairs or triads and charge them to find an "uncommon commonality"—something they all have in common that is *not* common (for example, they all have pet iguanas, they all broke a bone in their left foot).

"Human Bingo" Make a one-page Bingo sheet that has various middle schooler attributes in boxes horizontally and vertically, with a space in each box to write a classmate's name (for example, ___ has three siblings; ___ loves pizza; ___ plays basketball). Instruct students to stand up and talk with peers to fill out the sheet, reminding them to use each classmate only once.

Finally, students need to come to know themselves deeply. When a classroom becomes a place where reflection is not only evident, but also expected, students gain self-knowledge. Certainly the students with whom we talked seemed pleased to reflect on their school lives. Such reflection breeds self-knowledge—knowledge that enables them to assess their own strengths and areas of challenge. This can be facilitated through weekly or monthly goal setting, through personal learning conferences, and can be shared with others through student-led portfolio conferences.

The physical environment should mirror this sense of the personal. Looking around the walls of the classroom or team, do you see evidence of the community? A sense of what that community stands for and believes in? Clarity around community norms? Are there photographs showing celebration, and is there work showing pride in accomplishment? Are all members represented? Can each student find himself or herself in that shared space?

Create an Authentic Community

Students are astute anthropologists, observing and hearing everything that occurs in the classroom culture. Young adolescents know when their teachers mean what they say and when they don't mean it. They are acutely aware of the authenticity of their teachers' remarks. If adopting a curriculum or approach that suggests specific language or questioning techniques, like the Responsive Classroom (Charney, 1992), for example, teachers should internalize the approach and make it their own. If a discipline approach seems stilted, it is important to find the words that work and to say them with truth and meaning. It's not enough to seat the children in a circle to create a community; the conditions and tasks must be authentic.

Create an Overt Community

The students in our study expressed a relative lack of awareness around some of the very fine approaches their teachers employed in order to build community. The Morning Meetings and times in the amphitheater, we suspect, were precisely the types of attempts at community building we would applaud. Yet many of their students did not understand the importance of such rituals. Still functioning at a concrete operational level cognitively, many middle schoolers need actions and reasons to be overt. Naming, explaining, underscoring, and returning to the importance of coming together as a community create longevity and momentum.

Create a Safe Community

We believe that when the community is personal, authentic, and overt, it becomes safe. From a physical standpoint, students in such a community find themselves in a place where they and their belongings face no threat. But, psychologically and academically, the payoff is equally great. In a safe community, students know they are valued and heard, and therefore do not hesitate to raise a question, voice a misunderstanding, or wager an uncertain possibility. They are willing to try on an identity or an intellectual awakening, both of which are developmentally appropriate for middle schoolers. Through this, they learn. If a community is not a safe place for risk taking, the opportunities for learning are diminished. Like Shelley's poetry circle, an effective classroom community is one that is personal, authentic, overt, and safe.

How can you make your classroom community . . .

- Personal?
- Authentic?
- Overt?
- Safe?

The students in our study taught us that the social dimensions of schooling influence the academic engagement of middle schoolers. One of the central tasks of early adolescence is identity development. On that journey, middle schoolers are striving to belong, to fit in, to affiliate themselves with a group. Schools are one of the primary theaters in which that ongoing play unfolds. Attending to the social needs of learners, therefore, is essential to the establishment of the academic setting to which we now turn.

3 Choice, Action, and Relevance in Curriculum

Adolescents need training and practice in reaching intelligent decisions and in effective social participation. How can such training better be given than by group considerations of matters of as vital concern to them as what to study and how they will study it? (Kridel, 1998, pp. 37–38)

If curriculum, the content of what is studied, can be thought of as the *what* of the schooling experience, then pedagogy, the teaching and learning approaches, is surely the *how*. Just as our student informants had much to share about the social climate that was most conducive to academic engagement, so too were they clear with us about the ways in which they felt they learned best.

As students talked and drew about their experiences in schools, they were quite clear about the teaching and learning opportunities that enhanced how they interacted with ideas, with text, and with the teachers and learners around them. The educational community by and large has come to accept that there are multiple ways of knowing, thinking, and learning (Gardner, 1993). Beyond multiple intelligences, learning styles, and preferences, however, it became clear that the students in our study required ongoing and consistent opportunities to make choices about what and how they learn; they needed to be active in that learning; and they sought relevance by making connections between their learning and "real-world" application. Choice, action, and relevance: these themes, highlighted in this chapter, appeared again and again. They are critical to students' experience of engagement.

CHOICE

Students are rarely invited to become active participants in their own education. As Kohn (1993) and others have asserted, when students are empowered with choice and voice, their academic achievement, behavior, sense of self-efficacy, and understanding of democratic principles are enhanced. The students in our study also identified choice as a central contributor to their level of engagement and success. Appearing in a variety of forms, a student's opportunity to have a voice in what and how he or she learns came readily to the forefront of issues that mattered to these respondents.

> When do students have choices in your classroom?
>
> When else might they?

Linzzy, a fourth grader, simply and directly answered the following question in a way that mirrored many students' responses.

Interviewer: Imagine you have a magic wand. With this wand you could change anything you want in this school. One thing, two things, three things, OK? What would you change with your wand?

Linzzy: Umm. Having more option on what we can do.

For Linzzy, not "having more option" is the most central drawback of her schooling experience. Linzzy's picture of a time when she was not engaged (see Figure 5.3, page 68) illustrates in greater detail how a lack of choice can turn an activity she usually enjoys into one of frustration. She explained, "I think it's important to read a lot. But I don't think, I think they should ask us before they assign us books. It might be good for us to know about something, but I just don't like that we have to read exactly what they say. Because so far I don't have much choice."

Kevin and Carlo echoed the power of choice in reading, as they described what they chose to read at home, as opposed to at school. Kevin,

> When do your students choose their own reading?

whose experience of stark disaffiliation from school was represented in Chapter 1, mentioned that he often read at home, which was enjoyable "'cause it's something that I like. It's more what I like to do. Like these other books that you have no decision, you have to read them." At the time, he was immersed at home in reading about butterflies, a topic of great interest to him. Kevin's sense of powerlessness at school, that he has no decision, pointed to the need for choice in other literacy activities as well, as he explained, "Well, I like to write. . . . It depends what I'm writing about, too."

For Carlo, choice in reading was deeply embedded in what held real-life application for him. In his interview, he explained that he planned to drive himself to school in a few years.

Interviewer:	Do you already know how to drive?
Carlo:	No, but I'm reading the book though, the Driver's Ed one.
I:	You're already reading it? Did you just decide to read that or did somebody suggest it to you?
C:	I decided to, 'cause I wanted to pass it, so I started to read it.
I:	Good for you; you started early. Where did you get the book?
C:	My mom, she works for the town clerk's office, so she just got me one.
I:	Did you ask her to?
C:	Yes.

Carlo's initiative to seek out a text and read it on his own time is a powerful message to educators about the need for meaningful, real-world application in our classrooms. Equipped with the choice of what to read, Kevin furthered his understanding of and interest in butterflies; Carlo empowered himself with knowledge that would gain him access to a central rite of passage into adolescence.

Some students identified a certain time during the day when they could make choices. Nad, for example, while describing a typical day, explained, "Mr. P will let us read for like a little while and then he'll give us choice time where we can play a game. We can do work if we want to. We can maybe go on the computer. Pretty much anything that's really appropriate." Nad's relegation of choice to "choice time" suggests, by default, that he viewed his choices as limited or nonexistent during the other times of day. When Kevin was asked when he gets to make a decision about what to do in school, he replied simply, "Well, at recess."

Kohn (1993) warns against "pseudochoices," or times when students are led to believe they are empowered with choice but in truth choice is limited. An alternative is a balanced approach, such as a tripartite curriculum design (Stevenson, 2002), in which

> Are there "pseudochoices" in your classroom?

students and teachers share the decision making. In any case, the students in our study made it clear: choice empowered and engaged them.

Figure 3.1   Samantha's Time of Engagement

Figure 3.2   Samantha's Time of Disengagement

ACTIVE LEARNING

That active learning engages young adolescents surely will surprise neither the novice nor the veteran middle school teacher (Jackson & Davis, 2000; Knowles & Brown, 2000; Stevenson, 2002). Some readers may be surprised by students' awareness of their need for active learning, however.

Here, Samantha provided a student perspective on how being an active participant in the discovery of knowledge facilitated her learning.

> How do you organize your teaching to increase movement?

In the first picture (Figure 3.1), Samantha illustrated herself "offering to help find a certain thing on the American Revolution." She explained that she is engaged "when everyone is interested in learning and stuff." She eagerly discussed her excitement in seeking information and collaborating with others.

In the second picture (Figure 3.2), Samantha as learner was not even physically depicted, so detached was she from the task. In stark contrast to the first drawing, here the teacher's omnipresent voice from above instructs her to "open your textbooks to page 189." Samantha explained, "Well, I feel that when I'm working in a group and not in the textbooks that I learn the most. . . . 'Cause the textbooks. Some people, they don't follow it. They put stuff in words and ways that you can't really understand it."

Samantha's two pictures are powerful examples of her need for active learning in her education. In the first, Samantha was an active participant in her learning. She sought knowledge; she helped others; she constructed meaning through collaboration. In the second, while she chose to illustrate the same class, Social Studies, it is clear that she perceived her role in the

Figure 3.3	Anthony's Time of Engagement	Figure 3.4	Anthony's Time of Disengagement

 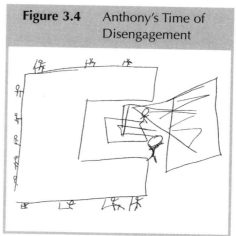

learning process, and therefore her engagement, as quite different. Rather than promoting active collaboration, the language of the text and the oral reading created barriers to her comprehension.

Many students echoed Samantha's perspective. When asked about times during which they were not engaged in learning, these

> In what ways do students collaborate in your classroom?

middle schoolers often described a level of passivity, a general lack of action, and often a reliance on either auditory or teacher-directed learning. Anthony, an eighth grader, offered two pictures that also portrayed these important differences. While Samantha illustrated, Anthony sketched. By most standards, Anthony would be considered less skilled in drawing than Samantha. The message conveyed, however, is no less important, supporting the use of drawing as an effective means to access students' perceptions and needs, regardless of artistic ability.

In the first drawing (Figure 3.3), Anthony showed himself seated at a computer, busily compiling Geometry theorems into one document in order to "prove by the end of the year that they are all true." While he did not depict another person in the drawing, he was quick to explain that it was a project on which he had worked with a partner. Once again, we note, the learner is central and the teacher not featured.

In the second (Figure 3.4), the students are seated in a horseshoe configuration, facing two teachers with an overhead projector. In describing the time when he was not engaged, Anthony explained, "We hardly had anything to do. We were just getting told all of our information. It's all lectures. You'd come in here and you did no work. You'd just sit there and . . . Some people would say, 'Oh, it's a really easy class.' Yeah, it's an easy class because it's so boring."

Figure 3.5	Jacob's Time of Engagement	Figure 3.6	Jacob's Time of Disengagement

Anthony's explanation that he and the other students were expected to do "no work" and to "just sit there" revealed the inherent mismatch between his need for the active construction of knowledge and the teaching approach being implemented at that particular time. His emphasis on application in each drawing underscored the importance of action not for action's sake, but toward the end of meaningful engagement in one's learning.

Similarly, seventh grader Jacob contrasted a student-focused time with a more highly teacher-directed activity to depict his requirements for engagement.

In the first picture (Figure 3.5), Jacob used color to represent himself and a peer preparing for a Science lab on exploring density. He explained, "You and your partner had to make a lab for density and see if water in its liquid state had more or less density than water in its solid state and you worked with balances and . . . we could choose what we did, to do a lab."

Like Samantha and Anthony, Jacob highlighted the importance of action in engaged learning. While their task was clear, the way of solving the task was not predetermined, and they could employ active and collaborative means toward that end.

When asked about his second drawing (Figure 3.6), in which he relied solely on black drawing tools, Jacob explained, "This is usually in Math like when teacher is just talking and we're supposed to be writing down stuff and it just gets boring and you just fade off . . . and . . . and sometimes he writes something with chalk on the whiteboard and we have to copy down what he's writing and he doesn't really explain what we're doing, so we're just writing down . . . Sometimes he talks like the whole period and makes you write down stuff. . . . "

Much of the professional development literature underscores the importance of active approaches to learning. Yet, the realities of confronting a large group of talkative young adolescents present challenges, particularly to a first-year teacher. Although more diverse, urban settings present challenges to adopting a more active pedagogy, we have known many teachers in large urban schools who implement active learning experiences. For example, group investigation of multistep problems engaged students in Math class in an urban middle school. The middle school students who studied the water quality of the Hudson River in New York became involved in the struggle to clean the river. The upper elementary students conducted a historical study of the block on which their school was located and designed presentations to teach other students. For them, the city history became real and exciting. It takes careful planning, good management, and administrative support to teach in this way. Still, we wonder whether the passive, repetitive practices teachers use are at times in response to the situation Carlo describes: the control and management of student behavior.

Duckworth (1996) posited that learners come to understand by being placed in a situation where they *develop* that understanding, as opposed to being *told* what they ought to understand. The students in our study would agree. The absence of the teacher in each of the drawings of engaged moments does not convey the irrelevance of the teacher; rather, it supports the current conversation in middle level schooling around student-centered learning as central to engagement. In these instances, teachers are facilitators rather than imparters of knowledge.

As with others in the study, Samantha, Anthony, Jacob, and Amelia (the students whose perceptions we have included here) described with excitement the learning opportunities offered and created by their teachers through which they actively constructed meaning, used technology, and worked with others. Perhaps because of these favorable experiences, they were able to contrast the others more starkly. These instances of engagement, characterized by active learning, and the examples of detachment, characterized more by teacher-directed activity, are clear indications of the students' awareness of peak learning moments, of the development of understanding.

RELEVANCE

Such peak learning moments appeared to be deeply situated in relevance for these students. Students need to see the connections between their learning and the world in which they live. Moreover, they need to understand how these concepts and skills have immediate application, not merely hypothetical future use. Well over a century ago, Dewey (1899) pointed out,

> The great thing to keep in mind, then, regarding the introduction into the school of various forms of active occupation is that through them the entire spirit of the school is renewed. It has a chance to affiliate itself with life, to become the child's habitat, where he learns through directed learning; instead of being only a place to learn lessons having an abstract and remote reference to some possible living to be done in the future. (p. 41)

In keeping with Dewey's assertion, Beane (1993, 1997) has claimed that the best middle school curriculum is based upon meeting the personal and social concerns of young adolescents. In addition, "making curriculum relevant does not mean limiting content solely to students' pre-existing interests. Challenging curriculum creates new interests; it opens doors to new knowledge and opportunities; it 'stretches' students" (National Middle School Association [NMSA], 1995, p. 21). Few would argue with the premise that students become more invested in their learning when it is grounded in meaningful wondering and is relevant to their lives.

Amelia, an eighth grader, identified relevance as critical to engagement, as she depicted two different classes and her reactions to both.

In the first (Figure 3.7), Amelia was deeply engaged in a discussion of Kafka's *Metamorphosis* after having listened to the story on audiotape. She sketched lively faces with open mouths to depict dialogue. She stated that this was the first time she had learned about the concept of alienation. Amelia explained, "I didn't know it was such a big issue and then I came into the course and then I realized that it was like pretty important." She leaned forward to confide, "Most everybody is alienated, so just, like, think how *you're* alienated."

In the second drawing (Figure 3.8), Amelia represented her Math class, explaining, "Well, I don't know, he didn't really give us a task, he just like was teaching us and then we didn't know what to like apply it to." With these words, Amelia highlighted both the importance of action (here, a task) and relevance (for her, application). For Amelia, understanding the relevance of the learning at hand was central to her engagement. For her, relevance came in the form of knowing what to do with the knowledge and skills she was gaining. Csikszentmihalyi said about teachers, "The more they can show the relevance of what they're doing to the life of the student, the better" (Sherer, 2002). We suspect Amelia, and her peers, would concur.

Figure 3.7 Amelia's Time of Engagement

Figure 3.8 Amelia's Time of Disengagement

STRATEGIES TO TRY IN YOUR CLASSROOM

What does this mean, then, for teachers, classrooms, teams, and schools? What are the implications of the students' perceptions of what engages them in deep learning? We include here some general suggestions for pedagogy, based on the lessons these middle schoolers taught us. Some of these suggestions will be familiar; the practices may be ones readers use. If so, great!

Create Opportunities for Choice

Middle school students sit at the brink of making many important decisions about who they are and the type of person they want to become. Within the classroom, making choices about their learning provides them a chance to exercise positive decision making in a supportive environment. At the critical point in life when they crave responsibility and independence yet still want to be protected, many young adolescents want to be trusted to do the right thing, to make choices that show they are responsible and reliable. These feelings carry over into their decisions about learning as well. Creating a classroom that offers real choices to students about their learning heightens the potential for students to be authentically engaged in that learning.

There are many models for student decision making in the classroom. Some advocate for substantial student choice in curriculum, like the negotiated curriculum model. Apple and Beane (1995) assert that democratic schools involve two lines of work: creating "democratic structures and processes by which life in the school is carried out" and "a curriculum that will give young people democratic experiences" (p. 9). Each of these emphasizes student decision making, and each is essential for engaging students in authentic ways.

An often perceived barrier to student choice in curriculum is the presence of state and national standards and the increasing emphasis and reliance on standardized tests as a measure of what students know and are able to do, in comparison to other students in neighboring schools, states, or countries.

Stevenson's tripartite design (2002) provides a helpful framework for embedding choice and maintaining teacher decision making. Within this "rule of three" (p. 161), Stevenson suggests three types of curriculum that are increasingly student centered. The first is "Teacher Choice," in which teachers decide on learning focus and outcomes, based on clear local, state, and national standards. "Guided Choice" is the second category, in which students decide from a range of predetermined options. And the third is "Student Choice," in which students decide based on their individual passions, interests, and questions.

Where in your curriculum do students find . . .

Teacher choice?
Guided choice?
Student choice?

Others call this model "joint decision making" (Grannis, 1978). We see many examples of the first two approaches in our schools today, particularly in response to the challenges inherent in a standards-based era. It is the third that holds the greatest potential for inspiring a passion for a subject in students and for offering students real opportunities to play an active role in their classroom community and beyond.

Embed Active Learning Approaches

Young adolescents need to move. While the nation's schools historically have followed a factory model (Grannis, 1967), with students sitting in rows and changing subjects every 45 minutes, there has been increasing acknowledgment over the past three decades that middle schools need to be developmentally responsive (Carnegie Corporation, 1995; Carnegie Council on Adolescent Development, 1989; Jackson & Davis, 2000; NMSA, 1995, 2003). Whether a school runs on a block schedule, with longer segments of time, or operates on a series of 45-minute periods, it may be helpful to envision the time students are in class within segments of 15- to 20-minute intervals. This does not mean that the topic or focus should change that often. On the contrary, long blocks of uninterrupted time enable teachers and learners alike to focus deeply on the learning at hand. Rather, middle school students should have the opportunity to shift gears regularly, to approach the content from a different angle and approach. If a lesson begins with a 15-minute mini-lecture, for example, the next 20 minutes might be spent in collaborative, paired investigation about the concept at hand on the Internet, through an experiment, or in fieldwork; followed by another 15 minutes of independent, focused work; culminating perhaps in the sharing of findings in whole group dialogue. While the content or topic at hand remains the same, the approach varies over the period, allows for movement, collaboration, independence, and focused talk, as well as a place for the teacher to convey information when necessary. We do not mean to offer a formula or prescription to a lesson; rather, we emphasize here the importance of variation and movement.

Similarly, active construction is a critical component of middle schoolers' acquisition of knowledge. Building in opportunities for regular fieldwork, experimentation, research, interviews with community or school members, and community service learning are all ways to enable students to be actively investigating. Schneier eloquently concluded that learning opportunities must be more than "curriculum as paraphrase" (in Duckworth, 2001, p. 78). Middle school students learn through the active construction of their own knowledge; we can heighten student engagement by providing actual encounters with the world.

Help Students See the Relevance in Learning

Providing actual encounters with the world around them also helps students see the relevance in learning. Carlo, for example, sought out additional reading, knowing it would help him learn to drive.

Engagement with the community at large is one way to bring home the idea of learning that matters. Service learning holds great promise for students to see the "real impact" of their work. Distinct from community service, service learning holds clear and intentional connections to the curriculum and fills a need in the community, responding to a mutually identified problem (Kurth, 1995). Kurth describes three types of service opportunities connected with service learning.

> How might your students engage in . . .
> Direct service?
> Indirect service?
> Advocacy?

First is *direct service*, through which students provide the actual service needed, whether it is measuring water quality in a river study or bringing lunch to local people who may be shut in. Second is *indirect service*. Students may, for example, hold a bake sale or raffle in order to raise money for a social cause directly connected to their unit of study. And third, *advocacy* is the work students may do in support of a cause, through heightening public awareness of the issue at hand or appealing to people with influence to make a change.

In each of these, the power of an authentic audience helps heighten the understanding of the work as important. It's not enough to have students merely write a persuasive essay, for example, that will end up in their portfolios. Rather, have students write persuasive essays for real-world consumption—the letter to the editor or to the congressperson. When students realize that they not only might be heard, but that they also have the responsibility to make a difference in this world, they are empowered in a way that occurs less often when the documentation of their learning ends in a folder or binder collecting dust on a shelf.

Relevance to the "real world" is important. So too is relevance to their personal lives. Helping students to find themselves in the content, to understand how all learning is to a certain extent autobiographical, moves them toward understanding its context in life. Just as Amelia realized the relevance that Kafka's *Metamorphosis* held for her, so too do other students want to know why what they are learning matters. One way to do so is to move from a topical approach to a conceptual one. Students have more room to find meaning and relevance in concepts than they do in topics. A theme on the concept of prejudice is more overarching and holds more opportunities to link to contemporary life than does a theme on the topic of the Holocaust. Though a class might study the Holocaust, the goal would be to learn about extreme prejudice leading to genocide. The Holocaust is the exemplar; with that emphasis students can make important connections to contemporary events (for example, Bosnia, Rwanda) within a conceptual framework. While a subtle shift semantically, the focus on concept rather than a topic opens the doors to dialogue about what's relevant in middle schoolers' lives, then providing a door to the tragedies that have ensued historically as well as in today's world.

Build in Collaboration

Most middle school students want to talk. We know that socioemotional development is one of the primary tasks of the age group, and it therefore also translates into one of the primary challenges of the middle school teacher. Finding ways to use the socializing for the purposes of learning is a huge step toward engaging the young adolescent. There are myriad ways to do this, but key to them all is actively inviting students to engage with one another in dialogue, debate, or knowledge construction around the learning at hand.

Cooperative learning is one very well-known method for achieving such ends. While too often small group work gets inaccurately dubbed "cooperative grouping," true cooperative grouping (for example, Johnson & Johnson, 1998; Slavin, 1994) is intentional on several levels. Orchestrated appropriately, it can provide rich opportunities for discussion, through careful initial grouping of students, attention to roles and responsibilities of group members, and, perhaps most important, individual accountability, a component often overlooked.

> **Cooperative Grouping**
>
> Have I . . .
> Identified roles and responsibilities?
> Clarified the task?
> Enabled face-to-face interaction?
> Ensured individual accountability?

Think-pair-share is another approach that responds to students' interest in talking while simultaneously offering careful, individual reflective time. Beginning with an opportunity for all students to think or write silently in response to a question or prompt, the teacher then directs the students to share with a partner for a certain amount of time. After each partner has shared his or her insights and ideas, the dialogue is then opened up to the whole group for sharing out. This increases the number of students bene-fiting from an opportunity to learn (they all think, they all dialogue, and

> **Think-Pair-Share**
>
> **Think** silently for 30 seconds about the question.
> **Pair** up with a neighbor and talk about your ideas.
> **Share** out with the whole group common themes and differences you noted.

they all have the benefit of hearing others' perspectives). It also guards against the traditional dynamic of teacher-student discussion, with the student who is quickest to raise his or her hand getting the only "air time."

Another (quieter!) way to capitalize on the social nature of young adolescents for the purposes of learning is through writing. Book buddies or reading partners have long been used in Language Arts classes as a means to have two students reading the same book dialogue about the plot, character development, or other literary foci. Having a journal that gets passed back and forth between two students for these purposes offers them a place and time to "talk" and promotes the objectives of the class. Teaching how to write dialogue through "note passing" is another strategy that students often love.

Design a Differentiated Classroom

Differentiating what occurs in the classroom based on individual needs, abilities, and interests is one of the best ways to respond to students' need to move at an individual pace. Traditional approaches to "covering" content as a large group at one pace does not respond to the idiosyncratic nature of today's classroom. Nationally, we see increased attention placed on differentiating instruction in order to meet the needs of all learners. "In differentiated classrooms, teachers provide specific ways for each individual to learn as deeply as possible and as quickly as possible, without assuming one student's road map for learning is identical to anyone else's" (Tomlinson, 1999, p. 2). In the best of programs, there are opportunities for student voice and choice in curriculum planning and differentiated instruction based on varied student need and interest.

Helpful Criteria for Student Engagement

How does the task offer . . .
Choice?
Relevance?
Action?
Collaboration?
Differentiation?

These students taught us much about the pedagogical choices we make that foster academic engagement. It is also helpful to consider them through the lenses of subject areas. Various disciplines offer their own unique challenges to engaging students in learning. Math's role in defining students' sense of self-as-learner presents particular potency, and we discuss that, and other challenges, in the chapter that follows.

4 Math Is the Measure

In mathematics, virtually every time you turn your brain around they challenge or, maybe better said, taunt you with a new potentially ego-threatening subskill to conquer. (Levine, 2002, p. 249)

When students think a subject is important, they are apt to be more engaged in learning it (Marks, 2000; Stodolsky, Salk, & Glaessner, 1991). Math seems to be emphasized more than the other "academic" subjects, at least among students of middle school age who consider it the most important subject (Goodlad, 1984, pp. 116–117). Students also consider it relatively difficult, some indicating it is behind only Social Studies in difficulty. When they were queried, fifth graders thought Math was difficult, but they preferred it to other subjects. It was engaging and required explicit teaching (Marks, 2000). When British fourteen-year-olds were asked to discuss a time in school that was positive and one that was negative, Math won with more good and bad stories about school than other subjects (Hoyles, 1982). Math was also more often depicted in student drawings of teachers than other subjects in Weber and Mitchell's (1995) report of students in Canada.

In our data, too, Math "won." Of course, we do not claim generalizability from our small sample; we do not assert that what was true for the students in our study is true for all. Nevertheless we noted many similarities to the studies cited in our students' drawings and talk. Our students also found that Math was an important subject. More of them featured Math in their drawings than other subjects. About half of the students drew pictures of Math as a time of engagement and half a time of disengagement. As we see in the pages that follow, several youngsters indicated that Math was a powerful determiner in their school lives. And what their teachers did or did not do while teaching Math mattered a lot.

In this chapter, we turn first to the aspect of Math implied in the title, the salience that Math holds as the indicator of how students "stack up." Most of our students seemed to perceive Math as computation rather than problem solving and critical thinking. We consider this in light of the heavy problem-solving emphasis of contemporary, standards-based Math instruction. The students described what kind of teaching is most appreciated and what is not appreciated. They commented on the kind of teacher-student interaction that made a difference to them. Finally, from these comments, we make some suggestions for practice, again modeling how educators might inform their own practice based on their students' insights and perspectives.

HOW MIDDLE SCHOOL STUDENTS FEEL ABOUT MATH

Math Is Hard for Me

Young adolescents have a very strong sense of their worth, or lack thereof, as Math students. Seventh grader Paula, on the question of herself and Math, said, "It's really hard for me and I'm not that good at it." Amelia (Grade 8) echoed this sentiment: "I'm not really good at Math to begin with. . . . It's my worst subject. . . . I just didn't understand from fifth grade on. I just didn't—I got it but it took me awhile."

Amelia's reference to her experience of Math, particularly the question of time, is echoed in other students' comments. They did not refer to tests or grades very much. Rather, Amelia and others had built a general view of themselves and Math. The students' self-assessments ultimately might become self-limiting, because when students expect to fail, or at least to struggle learning something, their beliefs can become reality (Cotton, 2001).

Two fifth-grade boys also reported that they were not good at Math. We turn first to Nad, who said Math was "really my least favorite" subject.

> By which subjects do your students define themselves as smart or not smart?

In this picture (Figure 4.1), Nad labeled his "Math book" and wrote "me getting impashent" to contrast with the "other kids." Nad explained with candor, "I don't usually get it in my head the first time he explains it." Nad shows that he needs several explanations to learn a process; again time is a factor. Nad presented his feelings about this in the drawing of himself looking down, hair mussed up, hand at his head, contrasting with the boy on the right sitting up straight, smooth hair,

Figure 4.1	Nad's Time of Disengagement

Figure 4.2	Lance's Time of Disengagement

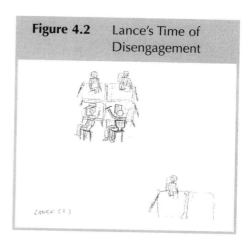

marking his paper with that prominent pencil, the boy who represents the "other kids." He depicted his intense frustration.

Lance, another fifth grader, summarized his experience in Math class and the feeling of being rushed. He explained, "All the kids are doing this paper so they could get out of class to go to recess . . . and I didn't know how to do it, and I felt kind of nervous." Not only did the rushed pace set up barriers to engagement and comprehension, it instituted high stakes: the potential loss of recess. Like Nad, in this picture (Figure 4.2), Lance contrasted his situation with that of the other students. While his peers all have pencils poised on the paper, his was the only writing implement to the side. The others were engaged; he was not.

I Am Strong at Math

In contrast, for some of the other students, the message was quite different; they had had positive experiences and had learned they were strong in Math over the course of several years. Eighth grader Anthony said he enjoyed Math, and when asked why said, "I'm not really sure what I like about it, but I guess I'm pretty good at it, so that's what makes it enjoyable, not struggling as well as enjoyable." We also asked how he knew he was good, besides not struggling, and he noted two important feedback systems: "People who have told me that, and I guess just moving ahead at rather a fast pace." Being told by others seems to have resonance here; even subtle messages from teachers and others give students clues to how they shape up. And in a subject marked by the progress of increasingly difficult topics, moving ahead at a "fast pace"

> How do we give messages to learners about their worth as students?

has substantial meaning. Laurie, a seventh grader who was one of the few students to refer to grades, also added another dimension: the social dimension of Math study, how her friends needed her help. "Well I enjoy it and I do well at it, like I get good grades with it and then also people kind of depend on me, like friends and stuff."

A sixth grader, Brian drew occasions in Math for both his time of engagement and of disengagement. Brian was a strong Math student, and this juxtaposition enriched our understanding of student experience.

After saying he was a poor artist, Brian turned to his picture about engagement (Figure 4.3). It depicted a time the year before, when he recalled a specific time and a specific problem he was solving.

"It's a whiteboard standing as you walk into the door. And I was doing this tax problem like 1629 times 8.5 percent. And I was doing it and he [the teacher] told me that I was going to be part of that group and I tried it and it worked out and I stayed there for the rest of the year. . . . And I was sort of ahead of the class and he told me there were three smart kids, very intelligent kids, in the sixth grade who were doing seventh grade Algebra instead of Everyday Math and he told me that I was going to go into that group and so I went into that group last year. I went into seventh grade Algebra. And it was really fun. . . . So I was really proud that I got to move on. And I didn't even think that I was as good as they were. And he put me up there and I realized that I could do what they were doing. It was great."

Figure 4.3 Brian's Time of Engagement

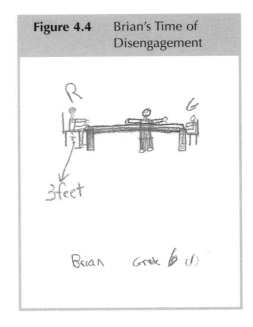

Figure 4.4 Brian's Time of Disengagement

Brian's use of words and phrases like "intelligent," "as good as they were," "proud I got to move on," and "up there" demonstrate so clearly how Math plays a role in students' minds (and often their parents', too) as the measure of general academic success. In most Math curricula, computational processes are organized in sequence and are cumulative. Thus moving ahead is notable and meaningful.

> What happens when strong Math students are not challenged?

Like Brian, many students referred to some kind of achievement grouping in Math. As Brian made clear, such arrangements mark students in comparison with others, and they reinforce student expectations. Paula explained about grouping at her school. "It's usually grade level, but there's another small group that has students that like aren't as—I don't know—who don't like learn as—I don't know—they're not as good at Math."

To Group or Not?

In his second picture (Figure 4.4), Brian depicted a very different experience with Math—one in which the grouping question emerges. The question of whether to group students by achievement is a difficult and controversial one for students, teachers, parents, and school administrators. Brian addresses it at a personal level. Though he had seventh grade Math in fifth grade, in the sixth grade he was studying the sixth grade Math. In a small, rural school like his, teachers are often unable to find the numbers to warrant an advanced class. In Grade 5, Brian joined three sixth-grade students to justify a special "class." Next year, when the others moved on to the regional school, Brian was the only one left. He was put into sixth grade Math. Brian explained what this was like for him.

Brian: Me and G are the top students in the class. And R was having a hard time with fractions so we have to keep going over, week after week, Math after Math. . . . He was having problems and Mr. K has to show us how to do it, and he keeps doing every Math problem because they can't get it and they keep getting the wrong answers. I don't know how they do these Math mistakes but somehow they make Math mistakes. But it's only reasonable to them they make Math mistakes.

Interviewer: So, this is you here and how are you feeling?

B: Very mad and bored because I just put my head down and I want to go to sleep because it just takes so long to go over and over and over again. But then after we get that done and I'm like, "Whew, we're done after like a half hour of explaining." But then we do another half hour because he doesn't know how to do like two to the tenth power. He gets confused, and I spend most of that time and he still doesn't get it and I explain pretty good to him.

Despite feeling "very mad and bored," Brian struggled with the concept of fairness, much as adult educators do. When we asked whether more help would help the weaker students, Brian had difficulty answering:

"Not really because some people get it faster. . . . Yes, I'd like to have harder Math. But then again I'd get ahead of the whole group and it wouldn't be—I feel like I'm bragging—it wouldn't be fair. I do a lot of Math in my free time and it wouldn't be fair to the other kids who've been doing really good in fractions and trying hard and aren't close to me and then we'd have this new stuff and it would start all over again."

In many ways, Brian's ambivalence about kids learning "faster" and fairness to others is similar to that many of us feel. Indeed, how a youngster learns to enjoy and profit from the challenge of a vertical curriculum while living in a fair and equitable classroom is a difficult problem. Ultimately, we imagine we would all agree that we would not want any other boy or girl to be "very mad and bored." Brian's needs could be met with differentiated instruction. In differentiated classrooms, learner differences are examined and form the basis for lesson planning; student readiness and interest shape instruction; and students establish individual learning goals (Tomlinson, 2001). Brian's engagement and learning would be enormously enhanced in a differentiated classroom.

> What strategies do you use to meet the broad range of achievement levels in your classroom?

All of the students expressed a sense that Math was something to "get," and the pace was of critical importance. As they see themselves "getting" new skills more slowly or more quickly than others, the students construct a view of themselves. The feedback received is part of the picture, too, even when teachers work to refrain from comparisons.

FROM PROCEDURAL COMPUTATION TO CRITICAL THINKING

One of the features of school Math today, whether in small rural schools or large urban ones, is the greater emphasis on problem solving. In the schools these students attended, modern Math programs emphasized Math as thinking and problem solving over memorization and computation. Vermont, like many other states, has promoted critical thinking in Math; its statewide Math Portfolio requirement in Grades 4 through 8 requires that students solve complex, multistep problems and portray their solutions with pictures and diagrams and written explanations.

> How do your students react to computation?
>
> To problem solving?

Among our students, there were very mixed responses to portfolio work, the part of the curriculum that emphasized critical thinking and problem solving. Fourth grader Linzzy relished representing her once-a-week Math Portfolio time (Figure 4.5). In her time of engagement, Linzzy showed herself at her desk with papers, the problem, and even a picture, her representation of the problem: Pattern 7.

Figure 4.5   Linzzy's Time of Engagement

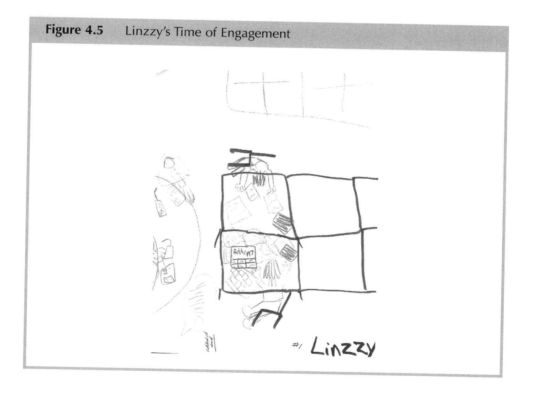

Linzzy placed the teachers on the left, not part of the activity. The bubble on the lower left with "Shhhh" shows what she told us: "I work better when it's quiet." Linzzy's close friend was across from her. We look down on both engrossed girls and their papers. Linzzy has lots of papers about her as she worked on Pattern 7. "Um. It's very challenging and I like to have a challenge. I like Math. I like how you have to do each step of it. You have to do a representation and you have to show your Math. So I make tables of T-charts or graphs, and I really like doing that part of it and not just think about how this goes into that."

With this last comment, she implied another kind of Math: memorized computation steps. "I like the Math Portfolio better than our um . . . I guess I just like doing the representation doing this kind of Math trying to figure out. Like I would still have to use the multiplication tables. I would still have to do addition subtraction but it would be in a different way. I don't really like . . . as much sitting down and having this huge division paper in front of me and answering all the questions."

Kevin, presented in Chapter 1, had a different response. "'Cause when you do regular Math you don't have to do writing and you don't have to do descriptions. I don't like that. You have to do descriptions and you have to do your writing. I don't like Math Portfolio. . . . Like you got to do writing about. You got to do a representation and then you got to do your Math and you got to do your writing and then at the very end of the school year after the writing you got your Math Portfolio papers are sent up to Montpelier."

Kevin had difficulties with writing, which interfered with his progress in completing Math Portfolio. He felt better about computation, however. "I'm not very good at Math Portfolio but I'm good at Math." For Kevin, and many other students, when Math was a matter of manipulating numbers, he felt successful. When writing was introduced as a means of communicating his strategies, he felt less confident.

The students we met in the previous section who felt they were weak in Math—Amelia, Nad, and Lance—all represented their difficulties in understanding or remembering the steps in computational Math. Perhaps this stood out in their experiences because it is so clear—one either can do a process or not. Whatever weight one might give computation versus critical thinking in Math, there is agreement that computation is a necessary ingredient to problem solving. In order to minimize the impact of the black-and-white nature of acquiring skills, effective teachers use a variety of practices. The students identified readily which of these techniques were more helpful and effective.

FROM CONFUSION TO CLARITY

Some of the students showed how certain teacher practices enhance engagement in learning skills. The students emphasized the importance of their teachers' clarity when presenting new processes. Direct teaching is critical to learning Math, as Stodolsky, Salk, and Glaessner (1991) found when they compared Math with Social Studies.

Clarity in direct instruction was important to our students, too, as seventh grader Georgia showed. In her drawing of a time of engagement (Figure 4.6), her Math teacher is in the center, with the overhead projector; Math examples are presented.

Figure 4.6 Georgia's Time of Engagement

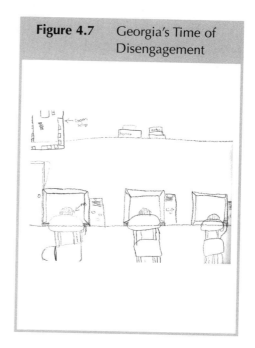

Figure 4.7 Georgia's Time of Disengagement

Georgia's own paper and book are included in the lower left-hand corner. When she explained why this was a time of engagement, she said, "OK, this is in Math. The assignment, like when she starts something new, she says we have to do it up here. And it's in our book. And then she gives us practice to do. And then that night we have homework to do. And here we're learning how to . . . and it's like decimals. And so she showed us like up here, the process. Then we have paper here, and we get a piece of paper. And then we do it in here. Know how to do it and then we do it, practice it."

Interviewer: Tell me about what made it so satisfying for you. Why would you call this a satisfying learning experience?

Georgia: Because she goes through every step slowly, so everybody can learn how to do that. So that I knew how to do it.

Georgia appreciated the repeated, deliberate pace with predictable components. These different levels of practice provided practice and feedback to the learners.

In the next picture, her time of disengagement (Figure 4.7), look what happens when she does not experience clarity: "The teacher Mr. B . . . and sometimes it's hard because there's so many kids all over and it's hard to see what he wants us to do. He does have an overhead, but you can't really . . . From the [problem?] on the computer and so sometimes, 'cause he has so many people he helps, it takes him a while to get around to you if you're not sure what to do." Georgia felt anxious when she missed the teacher's directions. A lack of clarity in the lessons plus the crowdedness of the class causes disengagement; Georgia's experience suggested that clarity and step-by-step directions are especially important in crowded situations.

How do you present step-by-step directions . . .

Orally?
Visually?

Relevance

For Georgia, Math was matter of learning and applying procedures. For more independent thinking about Math, students found other teaching practices to be helpful. One seventh grader had a good example. Here is Laurie: "We would start off with like shopping and that's what a bunch of like us to do, shopping. So they're like 'If it's 30 percent off, how much is the pair of jeans going to be?' And 'Would you go for that as this store has it for this?' And it was just like reality which was . . . That's fun to do because it's something you relate to even though it is in class in Math." Laurie liked the idea of shopping Math; it was an effective motivator to consider percentages. This was a fine example of how a teacher developed a good problem in which to apply skills, one that was relevant to the learner.

Alternative Approaches

Providing students alternative ways to understand and learn new processes also facilitates learning. Laurie was in Pre-Algebra. She found something in the interaction, beyond the particular program, that mattered. "I think it's also the way the teacher teaches it. Because I know like last year it's the same program, but last year I hated Math. And I didn't get it. And the teacher, she was . . . It was just hard because like you ask her something. She'll be like 'Read the book. It's right in your book.' And it's like we read the books. So we don't get it. And she'll be like, 'Well, I don't know how else to explain it. It's in your book.' And it's like, 'Well, you should know other ways to explain it. . . .'"

Here was some important information; this student preferred a teaching approach that offered alternative paths. Laurie went on about the advantages of experiencing alternatives. "Mr. D he'll do like . . . If you go up and ask him something, like he doesn't have to refer to it. He just has methods his own way which makes it so much easier. And like with percenting, to find a percent, instead of like doing all those division and multiplication stuff, he said just . . . and he turned it into fractions. And he just said, 'Multiply by that. Divide by that.' And go up it was like a circle instead of like all this stuff that was confusing and stuff."

Going Beyond the Text

Laurie continued commenting on how her teacher worked with the Math book. "The book doesn't always explain it well, whereas the other teacher, 'Yeah, sure, you can go like this, like this and like this. . . . I had a big problem in negatives and positives last year. I just could like not get it because she does this thing where like if you had to . . . You have to wait . . . If you're adding a negative or something you have to like . . . I don't know, it was so weird. I didn't get it all and like and we went through it every day. I said, 'Why do you do that?' And she'd be like 'Well you have to get a positive.' It was just like . . . And this year in Pre-Algebra when they put up any positive number I was like 'Oh, my God, do I want to be in this class or not?' And then today it was just like this, like this and like this, and I was like 'Wow, that's so easy.'"

With this lively chatter about Math, Laurie told us a lot about learning. It may have been that the additional year brought Laurie to a more advanced conceptual level that enabled her to understand positive and negatives more easily. And, as she said, the teaching made a difference, too. The teacher who offered understandable and alternative procedures supported her learning, as opposed to the teacher who remained too close to the text. Hearing about those alternative procedures, Laurie could move away from just memorizing the steps. When encouraged to talk and question, students show what they understood and do not understand. Explanation around different approaches would encourage student engagement and reflection.

Amelia, in her second drawing (Figure 3.8, page 37), when she was at Math class, drew herself and the other students sitting at a long table with other passive, unsmiling, nearly identical students, with their books before them. No one was looking at the teacher, whose mouth was drawn open to represent his talking as he stood by the board. Amelia talked about why she was confused: "I don't know . . . the ways he explained it was I just didn't understand at all. . . . Well, we have a book out in front of us and it's basically saying the same thing that he is and then he just says that this is the formula for linear graphs." Like Laurie, Amelia described a class in which the teacher referenced the text and offered no explanations beyond the text. Strict adherence to the text and its single process was a limiting element to learning.

GETTING MATH, GETTING HELP

How can a student who feels confused get help from his or her teacher? Amelia described her class as if there were little exchange between teacher and students. We asked why she did not ask questions. Amelia hoped someone else would ask her question: "Well, a lot of times people have their hands up. And if they don't ask my question then I usually ask it." And if it was

> How do you encourage students to let you know they need help?

still a problem? "Well, I either like ask one of the people in my Math class, like if a person gets it. And if I still don't understand then I usually go up to the teacher."

Amelia used a quiet, avoidance strategy to remain invisible. Only after trying several other strategies would she approach the teacher. We wondered if there would be a different story about Amelia's confusion if she used a more proactive approach to her teacher. She showed in this activity her need for direct explanation, to be noticed and helped. Would a clear, step-by-step approach, as Georgia's teacher used, have helped Amelia? Would alternative, more conceptual teaching about linear graphs have increased her understanding?

It is not surprising that, like several of the other students, Amelia represented Math as something to "get," something out there that must be acquired. "I just have to practice it, like over and over again." Later, she said about Math: "I think it's really confusing. There are so many different symbols, and so many different numbers, and so many different formulas. You're never going to learn them." The confusion seemed overwhelming to Amelia, but she really had the problems identified here. She indicates both by having to practice a lot and by referencing all the symbols, numbers, and formulas that she may well have a problem with memory for Math. Having to remember the steps to a process and having to remember all the nomenclature were problematic.

In addition to hiding her difficulties from the other students, Amelia hid them from the teacher, too. If Amelia were invited to talk about her challenges, if she could talk openly with her teacher, this problem would be in the open, and the teacher could work specifically on ways to remember. She could suggest Amelia develop a notebook of symbols and definitions, a summary of steps for processes, and the like. But, having used avoidance for some time, it is likely that Amelia developed skilled "pretend-attend" behavior to disguise her confusions.

Like Amelia, Lance also turned to other students first when he was confused about a Math process to try to "get" it. In regard to his picture of a time of disengagement (Figure 4.2, page 45), Lance talked about his feeling when he couldn't finish to get out for recess.

Lance:	And I didn't know how to do it, and I felt kind of nervous.
Interviewer:	So, what did you do?
L:	I asked Jimmy, my friend, for help.

Both Amelia and Lance avoided letting their teachers know of their difficulties by trying to "get" the process from sources other than their teacher. Math avoidance behaviors are rife among young adolescents who use various techniques, including passivity, to avoid engagement when things get difficult (Turner, Meyer, Anderman, Midgley, Gheen, Kang, & Patrick, 2002).

To whom do your students turn for Math explanations?

There is less avoidance in classrooms when teachers use questioning that supports and simultaneously challenges. Effective teachers encourage student questions and encourage students to take responsibility for learning. They model how to think through problems; they give mastery messages so that students learn to persist when initially not understanding. But when teachers do not provide these motivational supports, when they do not help students build their own learning, students are more likely to avoid mathematical tasks (Turner et al., 2002). Several students focused on times when teacher-student interaction facilitated their learning, and, through them, we can learn more about how teachers help students engage.

Timely Invitations to Learn New Skills

Fifth grader Amy drew a picture of the time, two years earlier, when her teacher interacted with her in a way that led to successful learning (Figure 4.8).

Figure 4.8   Amy's Time of Engagement

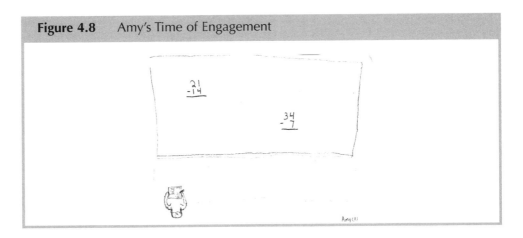

She explained how her teacher invited her to learn a new Math process: "And he said, 'Would you like to learn borrowing?' And we said, 'Sure.' I think I asked, "What does that mean?' He said, 'Well, I'll explain that to you.' And so he explained it to us and then we said, 'Yes we'd like to try to learn that.'"

Amy's teacher determined that Amy and the others were "ready" to learn to borrow and put out an invitation that engaged them. About a question she asked during the process, Amy said, "Well. There's stuff like. 'How am I supposed like am I supposed to subtract the number that I've just borrowed over or am I supposed to add it?' Something like that." And, with success: "Yeah. I knew I was going to learn it. I had kind of an idea of it but he really set it down." At first Amy said she normally did not ask questions, but then she showed how asking questions in Math enabled her to acquire knowledge of the procedure. "I just, well . . . When I don't understand something I kind of . . . I never ask questions about it. I just am sitting there. I'm trying to take it in but no one really notices that I'm trying to take it in because I'm just sitting there. But this, I was asking questions, and I was understanding it. And I do that a lot in Math."

> How many ways can your students borrow?

Amy remembered this two-year-old event clearly; she showed the distance of time with the perspective of looking down at herself from above. Engagement in Math was an interactive process for Amy as she sought specific information to understand the process and received it. She portrayed herself as constructing understanding of the Math process.

Teacher Redirection

Teacher redirection to new strategies also helped. Linzzy talked about that in connection with her portfolio presented earlier, when she had difficulty. "Well, we can go to teachers and tell them we're stuck. And then they'll give us a hint and they'll lead us on to something else. Like in the beginning of this one Mr. P said, 'I've got one hint for you. That's all I'm going to say. T-charts.' And we had learned T-charts before and that really helped." Linzzy's teacher judged correctly here that she only needed a hint to use the knowledge he knew she had. Linzzy was very clear about how Mr. P opened her thinking to enable a successful association to bridge to the current problem.

In another instance, Nad described a different teacher redirection (in connection with Figure 4.1, page 45). Nad trusted his teacher enough to tell him when he didn't understand. Neither he nor his teacher explored the details of his lack of understanding, but, in contrast to Laurie's problems with simply being directed to the text, that worked. "I said to him, 'I can't do long multiplication very well.' And he was like, 'Then you probably want to use the lattice method.' And he brought me back to a certain page in my book and it showed me how to do the lattice method and it's really helped me." Though the teacher referred Nad to the text, what Nad got from the text was an alternative process. This teacher seemed to have known his student well; certainly he responded promptly to Nad's individual needs. This worked for Nad, and he explained how to use the lattice method during the interview. He named the alternative process and thereby clarified the option.

In several of these instances the students asked for specific information or displayed uncertainty about specific processes and problems. Even so, the students did not always expect to get the information they needed. We know Lance felt stressed by the pace required to do a paper to get out for recess (Figure 4.2, page 45), and we asked why he didn't seek help from his teacher.

Lance: 'Cause Jimmy was closer.

Interviewer: Do you think she would have answered?

L: She wouldn't tell me the answers but she would tell me how to do it.

And all he wanted were the answers. Yet when students see the relevance of the task, they are more likely to spend time on the process.

Zone of Proximal Development

The students in our study painted a clear picture of effective teaching in Math. When teachers understood what the students needed, they were able to individualize next steps. They carefully and slowly explained new procedures and allowed opportunities for questions and practice. They answered specific questions; they redirected a student's thinking to alternative paths; and they demonstrated and modeled what an end product might be. When successfully engaged and learning, the students in turn reflected on their understanding and asked pertinent questions. Linzzy talked about how a "hint" helped her make an important link so she could construct answers. Amy seemed to know just what specific information she needed to understand the borrowing process. When his teacher suggested a whole new strategy to Nad, he opened a way to by-pass an unworkable situation.

These learning events are excellent examples of effective interactions within Vygotsky's (1978) Zone of Proximal Development (ZPD). We can imagine an "area" of knowledge or skill a learner has not yet reached. The ZPD is the area between where the learner can operate comfortably on his or her own and where the teacher (facilitator) helps the learner move further. In regard to the example of Amy, she could subtract simple numbers but could not borrow. She entered the "zone" of borrowing after first being enticed by her teacher; she moved into the ZPD through her teacher's modeling; finally, after her questions were answered, she fully entered that zone. With a bit more practice, borrowing would be in her independent repertoire.

To be effective in this type of interaction, teachers must know their students as well as Amy's teacher did when he invited her and others to learn borrowing. He also knew that among many alternative approaches, modeling is effective when combined with thinking out loud. He had also created an environment in which questions could be asked and good answers provided. Several of our students recognized the benefits of settings where such helpful interaction occurred.

> How can you create a ZPD classroom?

Creating a ZPD Environment

There are several factors shown in these exchanges that support teaching and learning in the ZPD. For one thing, in each case the teachers knew their students' conceptual functioning well. Here is where small classrooms have a clear advantage. In large classrooms, teachers use a variety of ways to learn about their students, and critical to their efforts is their creation of an open, inviting atmosphere that seeks students' honest questions. An example of such a class in a larger urban school is delightfully presented in Nicholls and Hazzard (1993). The more those students asked their real questions, the more they revealed their conceptual levels, and their teacher could respond. Many teachers work to minimize the power differential between themselves and their students. They seek their students' perceptions of experiences in class. These teachers are vigilant in asking not only *if* students answer problems incorrectly but also *why* they might have arrived at the incorrect answer. The answers provide hypotheses about students' thinking that stimulate appropriate help.

Moreover, as suggested by our students, successful Math teachers know Math well. The students showed why that is so. Teachers who are comfortable with the processes of Math can offer alternative approaches to solutions. They model how to solve problems. They engage students with relevant problems. We have seen how a hint here, the just-right question there, or a totally different way to multiply, for example, made a big difference in a student's acquisition of understanding. Teachers offer suggestions as they teach so students have strategies to build their Math knowledge. Learners gain in self-knowledge as they direct their own learning and "fill in" where they need information.

STRATEGIES TO TRY IN YOUR CLASSROOM

These students' experiences in Math suggest several classroom applications. We have organized the following suggestions into planning and presentation, interaction during teaching, and listening and learning.

Planning and Presentation

Planning. Effective Math teachers plan alternatives for teaching particular procedures and skills. They can be used when confusions arise, as Nad's teacher did when he told him he had trouble doing long multiplication. Alternatives can also move the students away from a simple algorithm idea. When students have more than one set of steps, one procedure, for a computation, they begin to understand that the processes are means to an end.

Naming the Process or Skill. When named, a process becomes explicit and overt. Nad's teacher identified the name of the alternative process for multiplying: the lattice method. Then, also, students need to name the steps to a process.

Use of Math Texts. Several students complained about their teachers' strict adherence to Math texts. Before turning to the text, effective Math teachers often introduce, model, and provide practice for the process being taught.

Modeling. When introducing a new procedure, effective teachers show the step-by-step approach while modeling how each is applied. By modeling, we mean that the teacher "walks" through the process, explaining his or her thinking for each step with imagined thoughts. "Let's see, when you add this positive ten to this negative five, do you add ten and five? Do you subtract? I don't remember, so I'll check it out by counting on the number line. I'll try to figure out what makes sense to me." In this way, teachers can show how they strategize in their solution to the problem.

Inductive Learning. Depending on the process at hand, direct teaching may mean drawing out from the students as they approach a new skill.

Practice. Before asking students to independently apply a new process, effective teachers have a practice period during which they keep track of who needs more explanation or an alternative approach.

Special Support. When students have difficulty remembering the steps of processes, it's helpful to create memory supports, such as delineated steps on an index card that the student keeps in his or her Math book, as well as offering broader, more critical problems.

Interaction During Teaching

Our students said that how their teachers interacted while teaching Math procedures was very important to their learning.

Learning Is Talking. Conversation about Math is vastly better than lecture, as Jacob showed us in Chapter 3. The talk is not only between teacher and student: students can talk with one another about how they solved problems.

Active Learning. When Math seemed to be exciting and challenging to these students, they had been invited into the process. Their teachers encouraged their questions, gave hints, and, in that way, brought them to understand new processes.

Scaffolding. In construction, scaffolding supports each story of a new building. In teaching, scaffolding means asking questions that lead to the next step in a process, giving hints, suggesting associations between the known and the new, and redirecting students into new ways to solve the problem. There were several examples of such interactions that illustrated the Vygotskian Zone of Proximal Development, and scaffolding is part of this effective approach.

Representation and Explanation. Math students increasingly are expected to represent their thinking and solutions through the use of diagrams, talking, and writing. Many teachers encourage extensions of thinking by having students talk to one another about how they solved problems or thought through a new process before they are asked to write or diagram.

Adaptation. If students are not strong in writing and thus at risk in Math when writing is required, like Kevin, further failure and discomfort can be averted when the teacher helps the students repeat what they have done into a tape recorder, listen, and think more about it. Then they can write using symbols and numbers if that makes it easier. Teachers use differentiated learning to heighten the sense of self as learner and to provide specific support. Students are asked to specify their own learning goals ("I will find a way to do long multiplication") in order to deemphasize comparisons and emphasize individual responsibility. Alternatives for reaching goals are provided. Teachers seek ways to determine how and in what ways students learn best.

Listening and Learning

Creating Open, Safe Talk. As indicated previously, strong Math teachers create safe, private times in which students can disclose their confusions.

Seeking Student Perceptions. Using this technique of drawing and talk can open the process of open and safe disclosure, if done carefully. Chapter 7 describes the process in detail.

Listening for Cues to Student Thinking. The more students talk about their solutions, the more their teachers learn how they think. Listening for clues about understanding and misunderstanding is critical for initiating appropriate scaffolding interactions.

Analyzing Errors. Rather than simply marking papers with right or wrong, teachers work to figure out how the student came to difficulties with processes or problems. We can talk to students about how they attempted problems to listen for cues about where and how misunderstandings occurred.

Questioning Behavior. Similarly, when students in Math class cause disruptions, it may be because they are attempting to avoid potential failure. Does the student understand the task? Does he or she have the skills to successfully complete it? Or, like Brian, students may be bored because they do not feel challenged. Is the task worthwhile? Challenging? Engaging? We do well when we ask ourselves why students might be behaving as they are.

Drawing on Different Skills. As we learned, Math is the measure. Is there some way that teachers can modify the impact of Math on student sense of themselves as learners? Challenging students occasionally to work in small groups or pairs to work on multidimensional, complex, and real-world problems might engage students to work together and to draw on and demonstrate different skills. A group of students called to find the area of a specific field next to the school or the height of the tallest building on the block will promote positive interdependence, and the student who feels inadequate may find he contributes.

Grouping or Not. Some of these students who are confident and skilled seemed to benefit from advanced study in Math. Others, who were much less confident, felt they lacked ability. Engagement requires that there be a balance of challenge and support. Some programs discourage homogeneous grouping of any type, but many parents and schools want homogeneous grouping to challenge all learners. This is a very difficult issue in many schools, whether rural, suburban, or urban.

Heterogeneous groupings can be used some of the time, for example, for the purpose of the complex problem solving described previously. Homogeneous groups can also be formed some of the time, so that all students are challenged appropriately and all have the opportunity to learn as much Math as they can. Thus, as experienced teachers know, it is helpful in this regard to change grouping patterns periodically. Flexibility is the key to grouping success, whether it is by ability, by interest, by choice, or by random assignment.

One urban teacher has developed a system whereby students become responsible for their group members and their own learning. Student assessments combine the students' individual scores plus the mean score of their group. After initial complaints about the system, the teacher found it worked well and all students seemed to benefit.

Downplaying the Salience of Pace of Learning. Clearly, the pace of learning computational skills matters to students. But individual responses to their perceived pace may interfere with their learning if they become discouraged. Effective teachers emphasize mastery learning and emphasize the use of computational and problem-solving skills rather than the pace of learning. They ask students to determine when they have mastered particular Math skills. When students are ready, they are assessed on those skills. While students will still note that some master skills more quickly than others, the emphasis shifts to one's own progress.

Over their school lives, students acquire a sense of how they stack up in Math. When teachers interact and engage with their students in the Zone of Proximal Development, when they create challenge and the opportunity to meet the challenge, the students show that Math classes are times of engagement. When there is little interaction, when only one method for learning new computational skills is provided, many students are put off, confused, and alienated. In Chapter 5, we find school experiences in Reading to be very different.

5 Reading in School

Reading should be conceptualized as an engagement. Engaged readers not only have acquired reading skills, but use them for their own purposes in many contexts. (Guthrie & Anderson, 1999, p. 17)

Many young children are highly motivated to read, but unfortunately, motivation decreases among schoolchildren as they get older (Wigfield, 2000). Not all middle school-aged students really enjoy reading, particularly, of course, if it is difficult for them. If students have difficulty reading, the older they get the more they feel it is because they lack ability, and they do not think effort will make much difference (Pressley, 2002). Such attitudes lead to feelings of helplessness about reading (Pascarella & Pflaum, 1980). If students feel helpless and not very good at reading, it is not surprising they avoid and reject it (Clinton, 2002). Yet it is at this very time in schooling that students are expected to read and study books more and more. It is therefore very important that we examine student perception of reading during these crucial years to understand motivation and engagement.

Motivation is a necessary ingredient for engagement in reading. When motivated readers mobilize their resources to read, they become engaged (Guthrie & Alvermann, 1999). Our students described in their drawing and talk several important conditions that led to their motivation in reading, pertaining to the text being read, the social situation, quiet, choice, interaction with the teacher, and individual or group work.

How do you increase reading motivation and engagement for all your students?

These young adolescents revealed a lot about reading engagement. Several students chose reading times for their drawings. Everyone talked about reading, and out of these drawings and comments came some clear messages about school reading. Two school reading activities were featured predominantly: silent, independent reading and oral reading. By contrast, there were few mentions of reading strategies and explicit teaching. Given the emphasis on direct teaching of comprehension strategies in education these days, we were surprised and probed specifically, "What are some of the different ways you read, in Reading class and the other subjects?" The first section of the chapter focuses on what the students perceived as engaging reading activities, independent silent reading experiences and read-alouds (teacher reading to the whole class). Next, very different perceptions of round robin, oral reading emerge. The third part of the chapter concerns reading strategies and literature groups. The chapter closes with suggestions for practice.

ENGAGING READING EXPERIENCES

Silent, Independent Reading

Through their drawings and talk, the students expressed key elements to their engagement in reading. For many students, silent, independent reading was common and engaging. Charlie (fourth grade) shows how common a practice this is.

Charlie:	We have silent reading periods in which you just read to yourself.
Interviewer:	This year?
C:	I've had it all years.

Amy had a unique way of expressing satisfaction with independent reading, or Silent Sustained Reading (SSR). "It's one of my favorite parts of the day." When asked why, she said, "I love reading to my head."

In the previous chapter we saw two drawings of fifth graders from two different schools, Nad and Lance (Figures 4.1 and 4.2, page 45). Though they were troubled by Math, they both depicted independent, silent reading as highly engaging.

Nad shows in Figure 5.1 what many of the students said they appreciated about this engaging activity: the sense of intense privacy and absorption when reading. Here he was nearly hidden behind his book.

"I like . . . I just like . . . I always do good silent sustained reading. I'm always focused when I'm reading. It's nice and quiet. I always like . . .

Figure 5.1 Nad's Time of Engagement

Figure 5.2 Lance's Time of Engagement

Some people are still . . . make noise 'cause they're like working on something maybe. And I always like to go to the quietest place in the school, well, as I can."

Lance appreciated the opportunity to read what he wanted. He depicted himself sitting at the table of desks (Figure 5.2). We see his back; his absorption is shown by how he has drawn his head down as he leans into the book. "OK, this is one of the first books I've read this year. Jimmy, my friend is over here. He's coming over. . . . I chose the book because it's one of the better ones I've read. Because it was kind of short and I like short books. It's a series book. That was the first one. I'm reading the eighth now." Lance's teacher allowed him to read several books from one series, and he enjoyed being "with" the characters he admired and returned to often.

> Do your students have opportunities for quiet reading at school? At home?

Laurie, a seventh grader, also mentioned quiet and choice as positive features of independent reading. "'Cause you can read what you want that that's what everybody is doing. You're not having to, like, concentrate from all the noise and stuff going on. It's just nicer."

Students appreciate selecting their own reading materials. A wide selection is therefore important (Ivey & Broaddus, 2001; Palmer, Codling, &

Gambrell, 1994). Here we note that some schools, especially those with relatively low funding, have impoverished libraries. Teachers can, and very often do, get books from the local public libraries. They also often buy books from their own sources. These practices are not sufficient. We need to urge school administrators, even when there are limited funds, to be creative and purposeful in working toward enlarging school collections. All middle school-aged students deserve to have lots of good books to read and to have substantial interactions about their reading.

Responding to Reading

A seventh grade student, Ron, said something obvious about silent, independent reading: "I think I like independent reading the most because I like not having to think of what I'm going to write down, like in literature. . . . But like in independent reading you can just like concentrate on the book and not have to like stop."

Having to write about his reading seemed burdensome to Ron; it interfered with the pleasure of reading. In her picture of a time of disengagement, Linzzy, a fourth grader, also commented on the connection between reading and written assignments (Figure 5.3). Linzzy was not engaged at all in her reading; she tells us that it was because she couldn't choose and because she had to do assignments.

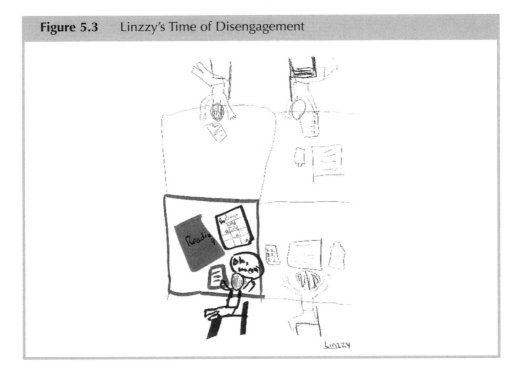

Figure 5.3   Linzzy's Time of Disengagement

Linzzy is at her desk with a book, paper, and a folder. Two of the other nearby students had similar objects before them, indicating these were common to independent reading. She leans over the book and her papers, saying, "Oh, man," in anticipation of a long period of silent reading. "Well. I usually love to read but, um, I don't but our teachers—this is our Bingo sheet—our teachers will assign us books that we need to read. . . . And I like sometimes I don't like the books they assign us to read. And that's when I get really bored because I'm reading books I don't like to read. But for like two or three hours, like well, like, two hours I'll be sitting. . . . And halfway through the book, they'll say, 'Do a book report,' and then at the end of the book, 'I want you to do a book report.'"

Linzzy seemed to have experienced the reading taking "like two or three hours, like well, like two hours I'll be sitting" and she reported having to write either one book report or two if the book was long. Though she probably exaggerated the time involved, her memory is of long, boring times with books and in writing reports. Her "Oh, man" shows the unintended consequences of having required reading and having to write book reports. What would happen, we wondered, if her teacher had talked with Linzzy about her perceptions? Perhaps he could negotiate a compromise approach that would engage her.

Under the right circumstances, students like to talk about their reading (Palmer, Codling, & Gambrell, 1994). The next year, in a new room, Linzzy experienced a very different process. "Well, one thing we do do is we conference on what we've read. And we do that. . . . Well, we didn't do that last year. Last year we wrote book reports. But, um. I like the conferencing better. She sits down. . . . And she asks you questions about the book and you need to have comprehended." Interacting with her teacher was important to reading engagement. At its best, as Linzzy shows, independent reading is enhanced by dialogue that challenges current thinking. Indeed, once she could choose her books and could interact with her teacher rather than write book reports, Linzzy could pursue her interests, talk about her reading, and be challenged.

> How might differentiated instruction change a "bored" reader's experience to one of pleasure?

Silent reading is not universally engaging or even challenging, however. While some students experienced pleasure in silent, independent reading, others, who find reading difficult and who avoid reading, may be neither motivated nor engaged during this time. Kevin was a student who needed considerable reading help, and it is not at all clear that independent reading was beneficial for him. His words suggested he was not focused during independent

> Is silent, independent reading productive for all students?

reading. "And we have free time, too, and we get to pick a book. . . . I'm reading a few books. There's this magazine that I was reading in . . . And I'm reading Daniel Boome [sic] and Lewis and Clark."

Kevin went on to explain that one conferred with the teacher when a book was finished; he said he had had one or two conferences with his teacher about reading. (This was late October.) Although Kevin's teacher was undoubtedly aware of any problems he might have, and had conducted other assessments, Kevin's lack of focus on what he was reading was striking. Rather than conference only when student "finishes" a work, regular conferences can track progress and provide direction.

Silent, independent reading was valued when there was choice among lots of books, when it was quiet, and when individual conferences occurred. When these elements were absent, silent, independent reading was less likely to be effective or engaging. Individualized reading is more difficult in larger urban settings than small rural ones, although we've known teachers who are very effective in conferencing with thirty individuals. Yet, clearly, smaller classes increase the teacher's ability to know students well.

> What positive features of silent, independent reading do you include in your class?

Another question emerges about silent, independent reading: Does it stimulate student progress toward the more advanced reading expected of middle and secondary school students? Some evidence, in fact, indicates that independent reading is not sufficient for that purpose. The National Reading Panel (2000) presented the findings of meta-analyses on the efficacy of independent reading and concluded,

> There are few beliefs more widely held than that teachers should encourage students to engage in voluntary reading and that if they did this successfully, better reading achievement would result. Unfortunately, research has not clearly demonstrated this relationship. In fact, the handful of experimental studies in which this idea has been tried raise serious questions about the efficacy of some of these procedures. (pp. 3–27)

Such research reminds us of the importance of a varied and balanced Reading program that offers a range of approaches.

> What reading activities do your students find engaging?

Read-Alouds

Read-alouds were common experiences for the students in our study, as Charlie indicated.

Charlie: My teacher reads to us and we listen.

Interviewer: This year?

C: Yes. All years.

Several others commented about read-alouds as a regular part of the day.

"We have lunch 'til 12:20. And then usually our teacher reads to us."

"*The Hobbit* and our teacher reads it to us."

"And then Mr. K reads to us."

"The whole team would meet . . . and we do like announcements and maybe Mr. H, it's usually him, he'd read a book or maybe a short story."

Knowing that read-alouds are common is one thing, but how and why do students value them? Teachers at two schools were reading *Holes* (Sachar, 1998). Girls from each schools voiced similar, favorable perspectives. Linzzy was one. "Yes, we all like it. We figure out all these things." Stacey was another. "It was really good." Charlie, when asked whether he preferred read-alouds to silent reading, really hit the nail on its head when he said, "Have her read it to the class. It's easier."

Most of the read-alouds mentioned were novels, but there was one student whose teacher read nonfiction. Shelley (Grade 8) reacted negatively to the teacher reading: "Mostly in Geography and most of the days we just like our teachers will sit there and read out of the book or something and it's just really boring

> Do read-alouds enhance your students' reading ability?

and it's hard to like concentrate on it because it's so boring." This reaction was not surprising; what was surprising was that Shelley experienced this textbook reading happening "most of the days." Ivey (2003) suggested that careful selection of interesting expository text related to curriculum should be used to demonstrate and model comprehension strategies, yet Shelley's perception served to caution us about the need to vary our teaching and learning approaches.

Since read-alouds are part of many school days even into middle school, their value needs consideration. Read-alouds do support reading growth (comprehension and vocabulary growth) for younger students (Dreher, 2000), but further exploration is needed to justify its daily use for older students, especially if it is not accompanied by teacher modeling, challenge, and thoughtful exchange. Yet we note that both read-alouds and silent, independent reading were appreciated by many of our students.

ORAL READING

We looked further into students' perceptions of school reading. Many of our middle school students spoke of oral reading, the kind of oral reading where one after another student in turn reads whole sections of text aloud. It was surprising to find so many describing this activity, as it has long been criticized as boring, anxiety provoking, and even wasteful of classroom time (National Reading Panel, 2000, pp. 3–11).

We recall Samantha's two drawings from Chapter 3 (Figures 3.1 and 3.2, page 30). They presented a sharp contrast between engaged reading and the stresses and disappointments that come from oral reading. Both drawings concern reading in Social Studies. In the first drawing (Figure 3.1), when engaged, Samantha was the girl on the right coming up behind the computer who asked, "Can I help?" She explained later that they were part of a group and were looking up information on the Internet to write reports and to prepare plays. The drawing depicted Samantha's desire to help the other girl find good information. The girls interacted around the centered computer. The other drawing (Figure 3.2) concerns reading orally one by one from the Social Studies text.

> Do your students find oral reading engaging?
>
> Do your students benefit from oral reading?

Samantha has drawn her preferred reading as a social event, as she and classmates construct their work together. "When I'm working with my friends on the Internet, I can talk to them and ask, 'What sites have you seen?'" For Samantha, reading for information is not only facilitated by the social interaction around the task, it is also helped when she can find several sources. "But once you like see it on the Internet on different Web sites and when you read it in different books, you kind of get to know it better."

Samantha made it clear that, though she reads a lot, reading aloud caused concern. We see the textbook reading experience through her eyes. We asked her why the text reading was negative.

Samantha: Well, when she says to open your books, we all have to open our books and just look at this and she asked someone to start reading and when you're reading . . .

Interviewer: Out loud?

S: Out loud to the whole class. And you think, 'Oh great, if I mess up I have to get every word right' and just when you're reading you're just thinking about yourself. . . . I think when you're researching by yourself and with your friends on the Internet, it's much more fun and this isn't my favorite thing to do.

We asked her more about the text reading. "It's just they put it in a way that's hard to understand it and so when you're reading you're like, 'Hey wait a minute. I don't really get this.' . . . I kind of read it like if we're going to have a test the next day. I read it again by myself and I find that it works better by myself. And sometimes I get confused. . . . I end up going back and reading it again and kind of finding where this paragraph where I need to read is and looking for the information I need. . . . But when you're doing this [referring to the text] you can't ask any questions. And you can't. . . . talk. You just have to listen to the reader. And when I'm just reading by myself I find that I can pay attention to the book easier I . . . It's just not fun for me. . . . And that's quite different, too, from the other picture where everybody is . . . like happy to be there and happy to help."

Samantha explained that the lack of interaction around the text involved in this oral reading was inhibiting. Like many young people, Samantha is familiar with and prefers using different media and several sources (Alvermann, 2002). Teachers are increasingly cognizant of this way of honoring student curiosity by encouraging autonomous exploration and group work.

In the round robin oral reading, Samantha found she did not comprehend well because the wording in the text was confusing. She said she would have to reread to prepare for a test. The act of oral reading and even listening to others read orally did not allow her to process the material as she did when reading silently.

Pace

Other students also reflected on the practice and limits of oral reading. In Amy's case, again in Social Studies, at first the fifth grader says she needs to do oral reading. "We each read a paragraph, or a page, out loud. And it just helps, it helps me because I've read a lot in my head. I don't read out loud much. So this is really . . . When I read out loud I kind of stutter and I kind of stumble over words and stuff." We asked her why she said she needed the oral reading practice.

Amy:　　　　'Cause I can read a lot faster when I'm reading to myself.

Interviewer:　Do you remember it as well?

A:　　　　　Yeah. . . . Well when I'm reading to myself, I can like remember. Well, I can kind of like have a voice in my head that it's the voice that fits the book. But when I'm reading out loud I can't make the voice that fits what I'm reading. So I can't remember it. . . . I'm kind of making a picture because I'm reading faster and I get what's going on, so I get the picture like . . .

I: You can't do that when you are oral reading?

A: Well, no, it just doesn't go fast enough.

When reading to herself, Amy applied strategies to aid in comprehension; she "heard" the text if she could read fast enough, and she made mind pictures. These strategies were not available to her when reading slowly and orally. Georgia, a sixth grader, also needed the speed of silent reading. "Because you can read at your own pace instead of having to either go too fast or too slow cause other people—like when you're in a group sometimes it will go really slow or it can go too fast where you can't understand everything that's going on."

And Nad had thoughts about pace and oral reading. "But if I go at my own pace, the books seem better to me. Because some kids in my group they don't read with any expression. And they read really slowly even though I understand that they can't read as well but . . . I really I like to just I really like to read alone."

These students need to read silently so they can process the material in their own language, so they can construct the meaning. Seventh grader Laurie said, "I tend to read ahead and stuff. . . . A lot of the people in my class take it literally, are really slow readers and stuff. . . . I love to read and so I just like to read right ahead and then finish it."

Why Oral Reading?

Why might turn-taking oral reading persist in spite of decades of professional advice against it? Students like Samantha, Amy, Georgia, and Nad felt held back by the slower pace of oral reading and, when reading slowly, they could not use strategies that helped them comprehend. Laurie just went ahead and read silently to herself. While Samantha worried a bit about performance, mostly it was the difficulty she experienced in the text and the need she had to reread to understand that concerned her. Amy needed sufficient speed to make images to comprehend. Perhaps if teachers talked with their students in safe, open dialogue, they might reconsider their goals for turn-taking oral reading.

No Oral Reading?

Would this mean that teachers should totally dismiss oral reading? We heard Jacob, a seventh grader, on this score. When asked about his reading preference, Jacob said he liked small group oral reading: "Just because I don't really like reading a lot and I can listen. So I can read and listen and do both." To meet the different needs of students we find in classrooms, could the class include paired or small group oral reading for students like Jacob, and for the rest, no turn-taking oral reading?

> Does oral reading play a role in your classroom?

It is important to differentiate between round robin oral reading and other kinds of oral reading. Teachers of young readers find that oral reading provides information for assessment. Teachers of more experienced readers also use oral reading in informal reading inventories and miscue analyses. These are individual sessions, and the process does provide good information. In classroom groups, teachers also often ask students to read short selections to prove a point, to provide an example, to prepare for some public purpose. These are fruitful techniques, and we recommend they be continued and, indeed, that they replace round robin reading.

The reading practices we have discussed to this point do not require direct instruction. In contrast with Math teaching, where presentation and discussion are deemed essential, the youngsters have not featured teaching of the same sort when it comes to reading. Instead, teaching was perceived as happening off screen, as it were. Teachers were in the background as they organized for silent reading, as they read fiction aloud, and as they set up turn-taking in oral reading. Teachers were setting the stage for reading rather than coaching their students as they did in Math.

WORKING TOWARD ENGAGEMENT

Teaching Reading Strategies

Though a strong reader, Samantha admitted to difficulty with the expository language of the text. Apart from the awkward and stilted prose often found in Social Studies texts (Loewen, 1996), comprehending expository text requires different skills from comprehending narrative, and Samantha may have needed help. Middle school-aged youngsters must read expository texts of increasing complexity, so the question of instruction in reading comprehension takes on some urgency. Though our students referenced strategies they used to comprehend (Amy's image making, Samantha's rereading) occasionally, it was rare. This is surprising because direct instruction of reading strategies can support older students' critical and analytic comprehension skills (Blachowicz & Ogle, 2001; Keene & Zimmermann, 1997).

Students' comprehension is enhanced when students apply combinations of reading strategies to understand and remember. Some important strategies include making images, using mnemonic techniques, self-monitoring, using graphic organizers, asking and generating questions, learning story structure, summarizing, and using prior knowledge (National Reading Panel, 2000). There is considerable value to be gained when readers predict, ask questions of the text, apply their prior knowledge, seek clarification, make summaries for themselves, and interpret for themselves what the text is saying (Pressley, 2002). And, when teachers model these strategies, help students use them, and use explicit terms for these strategies to encourage their use, reading comprehension improves (Pressley, 2002, p. 280). Ideally, the teaching of reading provides both the engaging independent silent reading and direct instruction in comprehension (Pressley, 2002). Otherwise, students will continue to have difficulty reading the expository texts they are required to read for all subject learning. The National Reading Panel (2000) agreed. And a recent report issued from the Rand Corporation (Snow & Others, 2002) called attention to this issue. From the Executive Summary:

> Research has shown that many children who read at the third grade level in grade 3 will not automatically become proficient comprehenders in later grades. Therefore, teachers must teach comprehension explicitly, beginning in the primary grades and continuing through high school. (p. 10)

Faced with this clear picture from the research, we expected to find that our students would make reference to specific strategies. In the second interviews, when we asked about reading, some students were hard-pressed to answer with respect to their classroom experiences. With fourth grader, Charlie, the interviewer asked several times about learning to read and finally asked,

Interviewer: Do you know how to use the table of contents and the index?
Charlie: Yeah.
I: How did you learn that?
C: I just learned it myself.

Lance responded to the question, "How do you learn to get to be a better and better reader?"

Lance: Sometimes Mrs. G reads out loud to us.
Interviewer: Anything else? Does she teach you strategies to read like in Social Studies?

L:	Not really.
I:	But when you are trying to find out about Egypt, how do you know how to read the textbook or on the computer? How do you know how to read to get information? And how do you know what's important information and what's not?
L:	Look in the index.
I:	And how did you learn to look in the index?
L:	I think it was from my mom.

At least one student did reference a specific reading strategy that she had learned in school. Laurie was not certain it was helpful. She described the process of doing character maps, for example, and following the plot:

Laurie:	I think they're kind of stupid, but . . . I'm fine with just reading it. And then that's the Heroes Journey thing. You write all the stuff that builds up to like the big climax, the big like frustration point in the story.
Interviewer:	Looks like you haven't gotten to the climax.
L:	I guess not. I don't know. I'm so confused.

We do not assert from these instances that the students had not received direct instruction on reading strategies. First, students may have internalized strategy use. Alternatively, the students may have possessed only a vague notion of reading strategies from school instruction, and they may have lacked the terminology needed to explain. Also, perhaps the students simply had not remembered instruction in strategy use. But of course, it is also possible that they had not experienced such instruction. Certainly, others have noted little such instruction as well (Pressley & Wharton-McDonald, 1997).

TEACHING PRACTICES THAT SUPPORT READING

We noted previously that students enjoy talking about their reading. Other students mentioned practices that engaged them. Stacey, the fourth grader introduced in Chapter 1, presented a different story, one that shows the role of her teacher in promoting reading.

Stacey:	Like in Social Studies we have this book that we read. And we have to answer some questions. And then when we read

we read silently separately. And sometimes we have like paired reading.

Interviewer: Oh . . . Tell me about that.

S: Well, like if it's not like a silent work time we get to pick a partner we want to read with and we get to read the same book. . . . We each read a paragraph. And we go to the next. . . . [Also] we have like reading groups. One group reads one book and the other group reads a different book, and we have to answer some questions. . . . We get like a packet that our teacher made us. For each book . . . We just read to ourselves and then we come together in the group and talk about what we have read.

I: What was the most helpful reading activity?

S: Like the reading groups. . . . Because the teacher asks us questions about the book. And we have to answer them. And we get more and more into it.

Questions are often merely assessment, but here Stacey described how the group talk around the questions her teacher had devised deepened comprehension. Such group experience can be accomplished in large classes, especially when well organized.

Linzzy talked in some detail and with ease about the role of good questions in her reading experience.

Linzzy: I don't know, she asks the kind of questions that don't really come out in the book. Like not [what] they've stated, "Treat was left by the monks under the bridge with XXX." Not like, "How did Treat get there?" They just came out and said that. But the kind of questions that were kind of beneath the surface.

Interviewer: Beneath the surface . . .

L: Yeah. You have to really understand what you are reading to be able to answer them. . . . You need to be able to really comprehend what you are reading to answer the questions because the questions the writer comes right out and says. You need to understand what you are reading and you need to figure things out to answer the questions.

In her way, Linzzy demonstrated the power of questions that require interpretation beyond the surface meaning of the text. Both Stacey and, particularly, Linzzy demonstrated thoughtful reflections on teaching practices; both had gained a perspective on learning. They, and other students, reminded us of the second graders Nicholls and Hazzard (1993) described as "curriculum theorists and critics of schooling" (p. 8).

Literature Groups

Several students mentioned Literature Groups. Although Linzzy was talking about individual conferences, it is quite possible, indeed common, for literature group discussion to engage readers in deeper thought. Literature Groups seemed to be a regular part of these classrooms. A fifth grader from Town School, Wildflower described what they are. "The whole group is reading the same book [in groups of four or five] and we all have different jobs. . . . My job right now is Passage Master. I find passages in the book that I like and I want to discuss with the group."

Paula reported on a Literature Group experience in her seventh grade. "Actually I'm in a larger group that Mr. A is teaching . . . but usually you just like talk about what's going on and what you've read like that night or like some problems in that chapter or something like setting characters and stuff." Paula's experience was less structured than Wildflower's. An eighth grader, Anthony, reported that students chose their Literature class; indeed choice is a recommended element (Lin, 2002). "Like currently the one I'm in, Mr. H is doing it, it's not one book. We're reading a lot of short stories. He titled it the Twilight Zone and kind of . . . We're working with human strengths and lack of human strengths." With this comment Anthony made it clear that the literature study was conceptually organized, another recommended practice (Lin, 2002).

In these classes, like Stacey's, there were a range of reading activities. When teacher questions spurred further thought, when Literature Groups were organized around roles that moved the discussion forward, and when the reading was organized to promote thinking about ideas, students were engaged.

STRATEGIES TO TRY IN YOUR CLASSROOM

In this section we draw on these student reflections as well as our experiences and research to suggest school reading practices that represent balance in the middle school classroom. The first part addresses the specific reading activities the students initiated. This is followed by a brief, specific introduction to direct teaching of reading strategies. The final set of suggestions reflects on the potential role of listening and talk that will enhance student reflection on learning.

Reading Activities

Silent, Independent Reading

The students appreciated the quiet, the chance to select their reading, and not having to write reports. Because of the need to include other reading practices in addition to independent reading, we suggest that 10 or 15 minutes of silent reading is sufficient to motivate and engage.

Many teachers attempt to work closely with parents to encourage a time each day for quiet when silent, independent reading is practiced at home. Specific times for sharing this reading in school create links between school and home.

Read-Alouds

We suggest that teachers read aloud, but only occasionally. These are opportunities for teachers to share special materials with their students. Teachers often select books and other readings that fit with current curriculum. For example, one of us read selections from Meriwether Lewis's diary when studying European American expansion westward. Sometimes books are selected to engage students in social situations, and the shared experience may deepen sense of community. Effective teachers use these opportunities to engage students in questions about the characters, the author's point of view, repetition of descriptive language, and other narrative devices. Thus, teachers model analytic reading.

Oral Reading

Round robin oral reading should be eliminated from middle school classrooms. Other kinds of oral reading do have a place in the middle school classroom. For example, we remember Jacob, who liked oral reading so he could "read and listen and do both." In classes where one or two students express this need, paired oral reading meets their needs.

Oral reading in individual conferences or with an informal reading inventory gives the teacher important assessment information (Stieglitz, 2002). Other oral reading activities in the middle school include reading a short selection aloud to illustrate a point, reading orally to answer a question, and reading to demonstrate. Oral reading of poetry is an art form that, individually and in group, students enjoy. One of us organized twenty-eight middle school-aged students in choral reading of poetry. We practiced and presented choral readings to the school.

Literature Groups

Literature Groups or Circles provide students with conditions that promote engagement: diversity of readings, choice, and student initiative

(Lin, 2002). Often students are invited to indicate which Literature Group they prefer, and teachers try to accommodate student selections. It may be the particular book that attracts students. Perhaps it is the author. Alternatively, it may be the topic. Often the difficulty level differs from group to group. In these cases, the teacher may assign students according to level.

As indicated by Wildflower, effective use of Literature Group often offers different roles to individual students to ensure student responsibility and initiative. Some of these roles are the Questioner, who ascertains that students have basic comprehension; the Passage Master, who finds interesting passages for oral reading; the Connector, who creates synthesis with other readings; the Illustrator, who draws. Students should experience these different roles. Sometimes teachers get the discussion started with questions they have devised, and they teach students to design their own questions. Often the group is given the task of making a presentation to their classmates, and here we are reminded of Samantha's group work toward developing plays. Effective teachers provide structure so that students learn how to behave responsibly in Literature Groups and to gain, together, in their ability to learn together and stimulate one another to critically consider the literature read.

> **Possible Literature Group Roles**
>
> - Questioner
> - Passage Master
> - Connector
> - Illustrator

We recommend that teachers begin each new group and use the first meetings to teach the different roles within the group. A primary task here is to facilitate student-generated questions, for good questions deepen understanding and motivation. Also during these first meetings, together, students and teacher establish standards for discussion and participation. As the students take on a greater independence, the teacher can withdraw and begin another literature group. Once the students are comfortable with Literature Groups, the teacher meets with groups only occasionally.

Assignments After Reading

A few students complained about having to do book reports. Linzzy identified a problem in always having to respond to her reading in the same way. In seeking more interesting alternatives, the teacher can begin by asking students how they might reflect on their reading. A brainstorming session on how to write about a book report would be a popular and creative way to handle this issue, and might result in some of the alternatives shown in Table 5.1.

Conferencing

Individual conferences allow teachers to keep close track of student progress and to promote deeper comprehension. To document the reading

Table 5.1   Alternatives to a Book Report

- Prepare a persuasive piece about a book a student thinks classmates would like.
- Write a summary from the point of view of one character.
- Compare one favorite character with oneself or a friend.
- Find favorite descriptive passages to read aloud.
- Write a new ending.
- Write a critical review.
- Prepare questions to ask others.
- Read a descriptive passage to the class.
- Find reviews of the book on the Internet.
- Draw a portrait or an event for peers to identify.
- Develop a skit from one part.
- Keep a journal from a character's point of view.
- More . . .

progress of all students, effective teachers of individualized reading develop a workable record system. Index cards may be used, one card for each student, or data can be organized on a computer file. These files track the number of pages and books read, oral reading facility with a small selection, the student's summary of material read, the depth of the student's comprehension, and how the student might share his or her reading with classmates. As we learned from Kevin, it is preferable to schedule conferences on a regular basis, regardless of whether a student has finished a reading or not.

Mini-Lessons

The Reading curriculum should include direct instruction on specific reading strategies (Blachowicz & Ogle, 2001; Keene & Zimmermann, 1997). There are many good sources for teachers to use to learn how to incorporate this into the classroom reading. In addition to the works cited, a particularly helpful workbook-like book is Hoyt (1999), which contains sample worksheets that are useful to indicate ways to plan the teaching. In planning direct instruction, teachers describe the purpose for using the strategy, and they name the strategy. They model its use. They show the steps clearly, step by step. They provide practice and application.

Sample Mini-Lesson: Self-Monitoring

Explain the Purpose. "If you are like me, sometimes when you are reading, your mind wanders. I'm going to show you how I monitor my reading. We have to first know if we are understanding before we try to do something about it."

Name the Strategy. "Self-monitoring is keeping track of our reading comprehension. It's especially important to self-monitor while reading difficult material."

Model the Steps. "For every paragraph I read, I will mark how well I have understood it. I will use this special code:
+ I understand; I am on target here.
± I am not too sure.
− I don't get this. I had better go back and reread."

Discuss the code and model it for several paragraphs.

Enable Practice of the Strategy. Supply a one-page expository text to practice.

Ensure Application of the Strategy. After discussion, ask the students to try it for a homework assignment, acknowledging that at first it may feel clumsy to use.

The mini-lesson format is appropriate for teaching all types of reading strategies.

Helpful Reading Strategies

Predict. One of the best ways to enhance comprehension, whether in fiction or nonfiction, is to predict what the text will contain in the next pages.

Questions. Teachers typically ask questions, but comprehension is enhanced when students learn to ask questions, first of the group, and then of themselves: "Why would the character do that?"

Connect to Prior Knowledge. When students are asked to link what they already know with the new reading, they make connections that will support comprehension.

Summarize. Throughout reading—paragraph by paragraph, page by page, section by section, chapter by chapter—stopping and summarizing to oneself about the content helps comprehension.

Use Graphics. Students often need to be directed to illustrations, graphics, headings, and subheadings to comprehend text. These graphics provide direction, and they also elaborate important ideas in the text.

Imagine. Making pictures in one's mind helps comprehension.

Self-Monitor and Self-Correct. It is essential that students learn to keep track of their comprehension. Moreover, there are a variety of fix-up strategies important to learn (self-correction, rereading, and so on).

Examine Text Structure. Fictional stories have predictable frames. Expository text comes in a variety of organizations. They need to be shared.

K-W-L

K-W-L stands for "What I *know*, What I *want* to know, and What I have *learned*." Learning to use the K-W-L process is important here. As students think about what they know with K, define their purposes for reading with W, and identify the new material with L, they deepen their reflections and ability to read expository material with comprehension (Blachowicz & Ogle, 2001).

Assessment

Students' reading affects performance in all content areas, and effective teachers are sensitive to meeting different reading levels with ways to understand the text. It is critical to regularly assess students' reading levels to ensure challenging but achievable texts for individual students. Generally students cannot comprehend prose beyond their instructional level, which is the level of complexity (grade level) at which students read orally with about 95 percent accuracy or higher, and at which they comprehend at about 75 percent accuracy or higher (Stieglitz, 2002). Below these levels, students may be frustrated and unable to comprehend the content matter.

Talking and Listening to Students

It is critical that we work to listen to our students and to encourage talk about how they read. One can imagine, for example, that were Linzzy to tell other students about going "beneath the surface," other students might begin to reflect on their reading. In one-on-one conversations, teachers might ask students about strategy use, possible confusion, and problem spots in their reading. For example, if Laurie's teacher were to learn that she thought character maps were unhelpful, even stupid, he or she would be in a much stronger position for redesigning instruction to show Laurie more about how these techniques could deepen knowledge of characters and character development. If Nad's teacher understood the importance of a quiet environment to Nad's reading engagement, he or she might turn more of his attention to matters of classroom climate.

Students' perceptions of school reading suggest silent, independent reading is engaging. By contrast, the students made it clear that turn-taking oral reading was generally disliked. Research suggests that silent reading is a helpful motivator but not a significant asset in gaining ability to comprehend, analyze, and think critically about expository prose. We recommend the direct teaching of reading strategies be built into ongoing content study; embedded literacy strategies are crucial to understanding challenging content area texts, particularly in the sciences and Social Studies. It is to these two disciplines that we now turn.

6 Inquiring and Communicating in Science and Social Studies

All knowledge begins in wonder.

—Aristotle

At the heart of student engagement lies an inquiry orientation. Hawkins's statement that "you don't want to cover a subject; you want to uncover it" (in Duckworth, 1996, p. 7) rings particularly true for the sciences. Both the physical and the social sciences are predicated on the discovery or construction of knowledge through active inquiry. The students in our study were full of insight regarding their study of these fields, in particular as they recounted their experiences in Social Studies, in Science, in an integrated Life Studies block, and in writing in these areas. Consistently, their examples of engagement in these fields conveyed the importance of "acting like scientists," of uncovering the big ideas.

There are three parts to this chapter. The first considers Social Studies and Science and how students focused on learning experiences

> How do you promote a sense of wonder in your classroom?

that were authentic and active. Next, we consider the role of controversy and discussion of current events in these content areas. Finally, the third section explores students' experiences with writing in the content areas.

In previous chapters, the students' drawings and words underscored the idea that active inquiry when studying Science and Social Studies is central to academic engagement. In Chapters 2 and 3, we presented many examples of engagement and detachment in the physical and social sciences: Recall Laurie and her Civil War timeline, in which a hands-on approach facilitated her engagement; Samantha's depictions of Social Studies and the stark contrast between her detachment brought on by the omniscient teacher's direction to the proper pages in the textbook and her active engagement in collaborative Internet-based research. Think too about Anthony's disengaging experience studying "explorers," depicted through the sketch of the overhead projector; and Jacob's engaging science experiment, in which he and a partner conducted a density lab. Reflect back on Amelia's description of the wave pool as an effective method for learning about how sound travels; on Shelley's drawing of the disconnected Science lecture and her elaboration about lectures, in which she expressed her concern that "they need to tell us information. But, I mean, they could do it in different ways." Finally, consider once more Carlo's comment about his teacher's response to feeling overwhelmed by the class: "She makes us open the textbooks and makes us read and do the questions." Each of these instances makes the point that, to actively engage in learning in Science and Social Studies, these students required a chance to connect with materials and ideas in an interactive way, "to be scientists": to discover, uncover, reveal, unearth, expose, and create. These students showed us that thinking in new ways and thinking independently engaged them.

THE INQUIRY DISCIPLINES: ACTING LIKE SCIENTISTS

In Chapter 3, we learned that students were engaged when teachers employed active and relevant pedagogy. We note here that these factors are particularly important to the inquiry disciplines, at least as the students perceived their school lives. They show us that active, relevant study enhanced their possession of the knowledge.

> How do you encourage students to pose questions and design their own ways to answer them?

Like many of the examples noted, Ron, a seventh grader, was most engaged when he was actively applying his learning. He explained his current study of the Civil War:

"Right now I'm taking a class on the Civil War and that's just . . . At the end of the class it's going to be really exciting 'cause we're like making rifles . . . because our teacher does reenactments so we know how to like—he knows how like line up and all the sayings and like the things that we're going to drill, I think it's like set up targets and pretend to shoot with the little rifles and stuff. Part of his reenactment group comes, so then actually that we're going to like—they may be able to shoot off the cannon if

Figure 6.1 Casey's Time of Engagement	**Figure 6.2** Paula's Time of Engagement

they can get it up the hill down by the church over there . . . and they're going to have the cavalry, which are the horses and stuff I think and stuff like that."

Ron's eagerness about his class came through in his whole demeanor. He smiled excitedly as he recounted the reenactment and the kinesthetic opportunities it presented. He explained that "I just am really bad with my dates," but he went on to describe how much he had learned from his attendance at the previous year's reenactment, where he learned "everything like the medical room and then the soldiers the ranks, and what they eat, like hardtack. . . ."

Personal Relevance

The importance of a hands-on approach to the sciences was echoed in many other students' examples of engagement.

When reflecting on a time of engagement in his schooling career, Casey chose to draw a collaborative effort to invent a future form of technology, in which he depicted its hands-on nature quite literally, and readily identified the relevance and application (Figure 6.1). Casey drew two students, side by side and busy at work on their computers. He explained the learning opportunity behind his picture:

"One of my friends had diabetes and we thought—we saw the insulin pump, which is pretty much state of the art and it's broken five times, but it's nothing when it breaks on him, it's nothing really bad. . . . It has over a thousand filters I think to make sure it doesn't break, but it still does, but it doesn't result in anything fatal or anything that could damage him . . . but our idea was, is, an implanted insulin pump."

As Casey described their work, his level of investment and ownership of the task became increasingly evident. Because he had had the opportunity to choose his own line of inquiry, he and his partner selected a project of deep importance and relevance to them. They went on to invent a new form of technology, deeply rooted in their learning and understanding of scientific principles.

Like Casey, Paula called upon a science example in which she found personal relevance to illustrate a time when she was deeply engaged in learning (Figure 6.2). Having traveled to the Caribbean earlier in the year, she found herself interested in coral reefs.

Paula: I was in fifth grade and . . . [I did a] project that studied coral reef and it was one of the best projects I've ever done and I learned a ton.

Interviewer: How did you know it was one of the best projects you had ever done?

P: I think a lot of people learned from my project and also I learned a lot and plus my report was really like, it had a lot of information.

I: How did other people learn about it, learn from it?

P: Well I had like—it was one of these projects where you had to have like a game to it and I had a game and it was like a card game, you had to match a fish with its moon and also I had like different corals that I had gotten because we went to the Caribbean and also Bernie gave me a lot of things 'cause he was really interested in coral and stuff and my project— like I have—I don't remember what I had, but I had a poster and it was really like it caught your eye 'cause it was really colorful and I had like pictures to it and stuff.

I: So this is the game right here? [pointing to the drawing]

P: Yeah, those little cards and then I had a notebook that had like pictures that I had taken in the Caribbean and I have captions of like what the fish were and stuff.

> How do you empower students to become experts and to teach others?

Paula felt this was one of the best projects she had ever completed, not only because she learned a lot but also because she found a way to teach others about it. She created an interactive way to teach others about a topic that held personal meaning for her. Like Casey, she had the opportunity to select her own focus, and the task involved hands-on construction.

Figure 6.3	Paula's Time of Disengagement	Figure 6.4	Charlie's Time of Disengagement

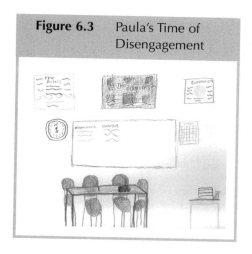

Passive Learning

In contrast, Paula and Charlie described times of passivity as their examples of disengagement.

Here Paula illustrated a time when neither the task nor the classroom conditions were conducive to her engagement in Social Studies (Figure 6.3).

Paula: It was really, really crowded. . . . You could barely find a seat.

Interviewer: How many kids were in there?

P: Twenty-five maybe, there was a lot of people and we didn't really do anything that was fun, they just basically told us about things like gave us lectures and wrote things on the board, like I learned a lot, but and it was basically from the projects that I learned the most . . . and you had to concentrate 'cause I was sitting next to all these people and a lot of people were talking and stuff . . . like, every day they would focus on one subject and they would draw stuff on the board . . . and then hand us sheets of paper to do for homework and stuff, I didn't really like it at all.

Whereas in her engaged example (Figure 6.2), the coral reef project took center stage in her drawing, now she used the chairs around the small table to represent the feeling of being squeezed into a small space. When probed about how this experience might have been changed for her, Paula suggested,

"I don't know, instead of having like a ton of worksheets, like maybe have more like small projects for this, but it seemed like every day they would hand us a list. . . . I don't know or like done different things where we—have projects that had to be hands-on or something and it was still crowded, but I guess there's nothing that we could have done about that because this is the only room that was open."

> How does classroom space dictate your teaching methods?
>
> How might you change it?

Paula registered her dissatisfaction, yet recognized the constraints of trying to teach and learn in a space not conducive to active inquiry. She points to a poten-tial limiting factor in crowded schools. While we have noted creative ways to facilitate learning in crowded classrooms (putting desks together to make open spaces for projects, work space in the class, use of auditorium and other shared spaces, lofts), crowdedness is a challenge to overcome.

Charlie too described his dissatisfaction with studying Science when it consisted primarily of passive learning approaches. In his drawing (Figure 6.4), he showed use of a video, and indicated which student he was by the inclusion of the star by his head.

"Well, this is watching a movie about the sun. That's some other kids like looking like that and that's like me sort of more like . . . like this is bor-ing. . . . They were just showing this big picture of the sun and they were showing where the hot spots were, and cold spots. . . . It was like review of what I did a couple of years ago. . . ."

Charlie's lack of engagement in a video that he perceived as review, accompanied by Paula's desire for projects, reminded us yet again of the need for active inquiry in the sciences.

Students are engaged by reenactments in Social Studies and explo-rations in Science in which they have opportunities for independent think-ing. Similarly, opportunities for discussion and debate lay the foundation for independent thinking. When probed deeply, contemplation of global events provokes the emerging and ever-changing thinking and identities of young adolescents.

Critical Thinking in the Content Areas

Since Plato, teachers have used discussion to help students encounter difference and to consider alternatives in light of their own ideas. One pur-pose for including discussion of controversial issues as part of the Social Studies curriculum is to encourage the devel-opment of critical thinking. Critical thinking emerges from the analysis of alternatives. By attending to critical thinking skills, schools can provide the common ground for thought-

> How do you define critical thinking?
>
> How do you teach it?

ful civic discourse and the emergence of the democratic ideal. Most read-ers will agree with the fundamental notion that schools have a role in the preparation of civic-minded adults. As Soder (2001) asserts, "It is to the schools that we must look for sustained attention to the development of the character of a democratic people" (p. 199). Discussion across difference is also thought to encourage students' interpersonal skills (Harwood & Hahn, 1990). Finally, through discussion, students learn to participate actively in the democratic process (U.S. Department of Education, 2001).

> There are those who say that young people should not take on social issues because they are not ready to understand the complexities involved or because they might become depressed. Such arguments, of course, entirely ignore the fact that the young are real people living out real lives in our society; many of them know all too well, from their own lived experiences, about the consequences of racism, poverty, gender bias, homelessness, and so on. (Apple & Beane, 1995, p. 18)

Research suggests that open discussion leads to feelings of efficacy, stronger civic attitudes, and more positive attitudes toward Social Studies classes (Harwood & Hahn, 1990). Political discussions, including those that take place in school, are factors that can influence future civic responsibility (U.S. Department of Education, 2001, p. 85). When students learn to weigh the value of different readings for their planned reports, reading and thinking are deepened (Guthrie et al., 1996). When discussion, alternative thinking, and respect for differences are not a part of classroom life, students come to rely on experiences from outside school to frame their thinking about controversial issues. As this occurs, they lose the opportunity to engage in discussion across difference.

> How do you prepare students to live in a democracy?

Discussion and Debate in the Classroom

We prepare students to engage in the complexity of civic life through thoughtful dialogue in the classroom. Students in our study experienced a range of opportunities to discuss and debate, from the highly relevant debates about specific school issues to the more global concerns of society at large. From cafeteria food to the war in Iraq, students held strong opinions.

Wildflower, for example, explained, "We sometimes debate about the food. Like some people think the food is really good and some people think it's really disgusting."

Carlo, now in the beginning of the ninth grade, connected a local issue with larger concepts taken from the curriculum.

Carlo: I know we debated on our rights in our classroom 'cause we're getting our rights taken away.

Interviewer: Tell me more about that.

C: Well see people, some people abuse the privileges that are given and then the whole class has to suffer and now we're debating on whether we should go farther and tell more people about what's going—see some of the rules. . . . Right now we can't even leave the classroom to even use the bathroom or go to the water fountain or go get our books or anything. We have to sit there for 90 minutes. . . .

I: So this sounds like a real student issue has come up. And who is talking about it and where are you talking about it?

C: It's mainly, it's not everybody. It's just our class, not the freshman class, that one class, C block. Actually right now in World Projects we're learning about the Jews and how God had made a covenant and I think Abraham was the first Jew ever cause he actually had a—I guess they believed that he actually had a conversation with God and when they found this box it had the Ten Commandments in it and there's a list of what Jews must do and . . . And what God would do for them if they do that and we made more notes. It's like what the students do or what the students must do. The teacher will let them do and we're working on that right now. So we're sort of debating on what the students have to do in order to go to the bathroom, but right now we're not even able to even leave unless the teacher is being real nice that day.

I: So that's really interesting that you were able to make the connection between what you are studying and your own situation. Did the teacher sort of lay it for you that way or did you make that connection yourself?

C: Actually that day the principal was in there just watching, just like watching the class and we were actually being pretty good that day and my . . . the Ten Commandments thing, maybe we can make one. And I told that to the principal of what the students can do and let the teacher to do. And she's [the principal] like OK so she asked the teacher if she could take over the class and that's what we did.

What are the connections between your content area(s) and your students' daily lives?

Controversy in School

The students considered whether discussion of current and controversial events belongs in the classroom. Wildflower said, "Well, where else are you going to talk about it? 'Cause the only . . . unless you go over to someone's house that day and start talking about it. That's not really something you want to talk about at somebody's house. So better at school."

When challenged to recall and think about discussion of controversy, several students mentioned topics that ranged far beyond the school. Many of these conversations occurred in October 2003 as the U.S. government contemplated going to war in Iraq, and the news was full of controversy. Wildflower, for example, moved quickly from thinking about local matters like the food to discussion of war with Iraq.

Interviewer: Do people disagree with each other?

Wildflower: Yes. Some people don't really care. Some people think that we should go to war because Saddam Hussein is never going to really get the picture. But my personal opinion, and most of my friends think this too, is that President Bush said after September 11 that "most of the children are safe, and I feel so badly for the children who have lost their parents." And we think, "Well, if you feel badly about the children who have lost their parents, more children will lose their parents if you go to war."

Wildflower had no difficulty relating what she had heard to new events, associating one event with another.

Students also reported discussing the September 11, 2001, attacks on the World Trade Center and the Pentagon. Linzzy, for example, explained, "It was really good for the kids to, um, to get their feelings out. And it went probably into December and every morning well like September 12 and for a few days after it happened. We sat down for I don't know, sometimes for three hours and we talked about how people felt about it and what happened and if it affected people. There were definitely different feelings about September 11 and what we should do about it."

Amy brought up the presidential election of 2000 and, in her comments, showed the importance of political talk for shaping how to disagree and how others think.

Amy: I remember when I was in the fourth grade, we were discussing about the election and um people were discussing whether they wanted Bush or Gore or Nader to win. Most of the boys were saying they wanted Bush to win because

> Gore was going to say, he was going to take away guns or something. . . . And most of the girls were saying, "That's not a big deal."
>
> Like their parents thought that it would be more reasonable for . . . They were going along with their parents, what their parents thought. And a couple of people who . . . I don't know I think they thought that. Well it was just a big discussion and everyone was talking about it. And everyone was saying, "No I want him to win." "No, I want him."

Interviewer: Do you think those kinds of conversations belong in school?

A: Yes, I think they do. I think you shouldn't just discuss school, what's going on in school, but like things that are going on in the world.

We asked Amy why controversy and current events belonged in school. Amy was quite thoughtful:

A: Well, to get other people's opinions. And to see other perspectives of it. And just to share your feelings about it.

I: What does that do to your own thinking when you hear somebody else with a different point of view?

A: Well, sometimes it depends on the other person's point of view. Because if it's about taking away guns, it doesn't change my thinking at all. But if it's a reasonable opinion, like it's something that makes sense, I might look at it that way and just think about it and decide if it's really what I really want to think about. . . .

Amy felt she would hold to basic beliefs but would be willing to listen and consider alternatives. At the same time, she was clear that she would not change her mind without further thought. Amy's awareness that controversy exposed her to others' perspectives is a crucial point in teaching critical thinking to young adolescents. Introduced at a time of pivotal moral development and the emergence of abstract thought, discussion and debate can provide an important mechanism to assisting students in identifying a problem, weighing alternatives and contrary facts and opinions, and developing a position.

Similarly, Kevin had strongly held ideas.

Kevin: Well we have talked kind of about that, like if war is a good thing or not. And some people said yes and some people said no. I said yes because like war . . . It's a bad thing, but if we didn't have like if we said that we should have peace and other people said that they should fight. When they fight, we're just going to be like sitting ducks. We're not going to be ready or anything.

Interviewer: What do you think of somebody who doesn't have your opinion?

K: That it's their opinion and it's OK.

I: Does it help to hear other people's opinions?

K: Yeah. Like if I get a reason why people don't like war then it helps me decide more on what I like. . . . It's not like I'm going to go with someone who is wrong, but if I see that like somebody is saying that war is bad and a lot of people are saying that war is bad. But like I don't then say that war is bad. Like I need a reason.

Linzzy also favored open discussion.

Interviewer: Do you think it's important to get the opinions out in the air?

Linzzy: Yeah. If people don't do like, "No, I'm right." But yeah, I do. Everybody does have their own opinion so I think it's good to even if other people don't agree with you. You still have a right to have an opinion. Yeah. Other people can know your opinion but they don't have to agree. But they can know that. That's not good to just also have the teacher tell you everything. We do a lot of that. I've always done that with all the teachers. It's not just the teacher, it's the kids working together to do things.

These students have expressed what is important in discussion. They have shown that others' opinions need to be heard. When reasonable explanations are at hand, they asserted that they would think critically and possibly change their positions. As young adolescents, they have an emerging understanding of the complexity of moral issues and begin to consider a grey area, no longer seeing everything in black and white. Linzzy understood the importance of not relying only on the teacher's telling but instead constructing together their reactions to important issues. These young students offered good reasons for embarking on discussion of controversial issues as groups of adults would. At their most reflective, the students saw this as an opportunity to reconsider, to analyze, to think critically.

A Cautionary Note

Though they made it clear that open, thoughtful discussion is important to encourage deeper considerations, students' comments also served to caution. It is not necessarily easy to create the safe zone required for talk about controversial issues. Because young adolescence can be a time when youngsters judge others quickly, but acknowledge their own faults slowly, it is crucial to create norms that help students engage in positive disagreement. For example, when recalling a debate on abortion, seventh grader Paula said, "It was just like crazy cause a lot of people were on like different sides and we were trying to debate it like organize . . . didn't seem very organized cause a lot of people were yelling and stuff." And, in addition to organization of talk, she said something else that suggested teachers must consider student safety: "Well, I know when I was in fifth grade I was kind of scared to like speak up because I was afraid that people would call me like stupid or something."

Charlie was also attentive to hurting feelings when considering the role of controversy in school. When asked if school is the place to have arguments or discussions, he replied,

Charlie: No . . . because you can get into trouble.

Interviewer: How? I mean what if you and some others disagreed about whether we should go to war against Iraq, for example, would that get you into trouble?

C: No, but we're not supposed to talk about that stuff in school.

I: Why?

C: Because maybe some people's families live in Iraq or something.

Charlie was mindful of the potential challenges of disagreement in school.

His clear words that "we're not supposed to talk about that stuff in school" deny the role of schooling to shape political thinking. Georgia shared Charlie's concerns:

"When people disagree, Mr. D usually stops them, but sometimes he jumps in on it and gives his opinion, which is good. Because it might go too far and it's something, I don't know, maybe it's just out of control and maybe something that shouldn't be talked about, like sex."

Regardless of their beliefs about the role of controversy in school, students agreed that the climate of the discussion was essential. When discussion of controversial issues is organized so that students reach beyond bickering, and when the topics are of deep concern, safe discussion can be a strong vehicle to promotion of critical thinking. In such circumstances, teachers' views take a back seat and, as Linzzy said, are replaced by the "kids working together." Although most of our students' experiences with debate occurred within Social Studies, similar, rich opportunities lie within the study of Science as well. These young people seem to confirm what the research sug-

> What issues are considered "fair game" in your classroom?
>
> What group norms help students know how to disagree respectfully?

gests: talk about controversial, current political and scientific issues in school carries the potential for deepening students' thinking and for preparing civic-minded citizens of a democracy.

ON WRITING IN THE CONTENT AREAS

Critical thinking skills can also be embedded in writing programs and assignments, as a vehicle for furthering both abstract thought and writing skills. It hasn't always been that way. If the students of 30 or 40 years ago looked in to see how today's students write in school, they would be amazed. They would see a greater emphasis on the process of writing instead of the perfection of the product. They would see students writing on their chosen topics, turning to their friends

> What is the link between critical thinking and writing?

and the teacher for editing, redrafting, sharing, and publishing. Students would be using computers to compose and revise. Students might coauthor papers and talk with one another about important writing issues such as audience. They would be writing in logs and journals to inform themselves and their teachers about what they understand even outside of the Language Arts classroom.

According to professional literature, these activities are not uncommon to upper grade and middle school classrooms (Farnan & Dahl, 2003; Simmons & Carroll, 2003; Smith, 2000). But is it realistic to expect these activities in classrooms when external demands, such as preparation for standardized tests, constrain instructional time? How do students feel about the variety of approaches to writing? As our students talked about writing in the content areas, three themes emerged. First, they described various experiences with journals and learning logs, approaches that provide "writing to learn" opportunities. Second, they detailed their experiences with technology in the writing process. Finally, we heard about the role of feedback and assessment in writing.

Writing to Learn

For many students, writing can help refine their thinking and formation of ideas. Atwell (1990) recommended that writing process activities be used to help students learn in the content areas. Amelia illustrated the power of writing to learn when she explained, "Well like I know 'cause we had to do this write-up about what we learned after and then I didn't think I learned that much, but then I just wrote about all these things and it was a pretty long paper." This eighth grader learned that writing "up about what we learned" was a way of recalling and, possibly, restructuring her learning.

The use of journals and learning logs can be another less formal strategy to stimulate learning through writing. Atwell (1990) suggested that students respond in logs for 10 focused minutes to teacher prompts. Learning logs have been used as a bridge from the writing of narrative to writing in the content areas (Collins, 1990). Logs can be used to inform teachers on their students' understanding before, during, and after instruction in the content areas (Chard, 1990). Linzzy described her use of learning logs in two areas:

Linzzy:	And then we have a writing log. Which I love to write also. And I'm like we can all write a story. And I'm writing a diary.
Interviewer:	A real diary?
L:	Well, it's fiction. It's not about me. So we have that and we have our log for Inquiry.

Although Linzzy described her success with this activity, Kevin, the fourth grader introduced in Chapter 1, expressed his concerns about writing. In his drawing (Figure 1.2, page 6), Kevin showed his pencil lying next to the journal he is reaching for. Kevin struggled with writing and said, quite plainly, "I don't like to write in my journal." We asked how the journal writing was set up, he explained:

Kevin:	On the chalkboard you have they write up a sentence and you have to think of something to go with that sentence.
Interviewer:	Oh, can you give an example?
K:	"The bus came to an abrupt stop."
I:	What did you write about with that one?
K:	"And the kids came tumbling out." I don't think I was very descriptive. I wrote down that and I couldn't think of anything else.

Smith (2000) suggested that journal writing is a good way to begin writing workshop or process writing, because it enhances fluency. But Kevin seemed to experience severe limits to writing fluency.

Interviewer: You don't think you are a good writer? Why do you think that?

Kevin: Because it takes me way too long to get it done. And I'm still doing it and everybody else is done and doing something else.

Kevin related pace with success. In addition to worries about fluency, students like Kevin may not value journal writing if there is not sufficient attention paid to it.

I: And what happens to your journal after you write in it. Where do you put it?

K: In my desk.

I: And who reads it?

K: I do.

I: Do the teachers read it?

K: No.

Though Kevin called this a journal, it is not the personal, free writing that one usually thinks of as journal writing. Instead it is more like a learning log, where teachers provide prompts from which students write. Kevin's awareness of the lack of audience is a reminder of the importance of audience in writing. While obviously balance is important, students like Kevin who

> Who is the audience for your students' work?
>
> How does it vary based on task?

struggle with writing need to see the value and relevance in the writing task. Writing in the content areas may provide a way for teachers and students to communicate (Sensenbaugh, 1993) as well as assist in the acquisition of new concepts, but only when students feel a true sense of investment.

Writing and Technology

Another component of contemporary school writing is the use of technology. The ability to use the computer ought to enhance fluency, but it is not altogether clear whether word processing supports writing (Farnan & Dahl, 2003): "We have yet to experience a generation of children whose main writing tool is the computer and whose revision strategies include such computer manipulations as merging drafts, moving text, deleting, and printing out alternative versions" (p. 999).

Indeed, as our students told us, composing was still mostly a paper-and-pen matter. Georgia explained a bit about writing in Grade 6. "In writing, everybody has their own story. Different people are on the computers typing it. Different people are writing by hand." Later she explained the difference. "We use the computers for typing up our writing." Another sixth grader, Brian, explained:

Brian:	We can choose like reading or writing and sometimes we do typing in there.
Interviewer:	On the computer?
B:	Yeah. 'Cause we do rough drafts on paper and then on the computer we type.
I:	Have you ever written your rough draft on the computer?
B:	No.

When writers, including young students, compose on the computer, revisions are made during the initial drafting, and the quality improves (Farnan & Dahl, 2003). Yet one of the biggest challenges to technology advancement in classrooms is lack of adequate resources. Georgia and Brian may not be composing on the computer because their schools do not have enough computers. If they have computer availability at home, they will be able to practice and become proficient at keyboarding and thereby enjoy the flexibility of word-processing composing. Of course, not all students have computers at home. While the resource gap between schools, based on social class and ethnicity, that existed 10 years ago has dropped significantly, the divide by family wealth in terms of home computers and Internet linkup continues (*Education Week*, 2004).

> What role(s) can computers play in the composition process?

An alternative writing experience using the computer was portrayed in Stacey's description of the PowerPoint presentation she was preparing, as shown in the picture in Figure 1.1 (page 6). Stacey enjoyed the process so much she remembered the exact words used on a slide.

Stacey:	It says, "Michael Jordan can make slam dunks and sometimes when he makes slam dunks he makes funny faces. . . ."
Interviewer:	So your slides are your own words that you remember from the book?
S:	Something that tells us in the book but we put in our own words.

Stacey's school possessed sets of laptops for whole classes. This investment made it possible for equitable use of resources and the possibility for multimedia work.

Teacher Feedback and Self-Assessment

In addition to these experiences in writing, the students spoke to the ways in which they experienced feedback and assessment. Although the traditional method of teacher corrections on student papers has not been found to improve writing (Hillocks, 1986), Casey, a seventh grader, appreciated it very much.

> What forms of assessment do students receive from you?
>
> From peers?
>
> From themselves?

Interviewer: How does the teacher work with you in writing, when you were struggling on this piece?

Casey: Mr. H gives like ideas for improvement and writes all over telling you what you need to improve and then really just helps out with it.

Jacob, on the other hand, reported some frustration with such corrections. When he and a classmate were working on a Science lab "we kept messing up, typing it up."

Interviewer: Talk to me about how you kept messing up when you were typing it up.

Jacob: Well we typed. We talked to our teacher about it. Then he'd tell us what to fix on it, and we go type it up. Then we'd go back to him and we did something wrong. I think we mistyped something, so we had to go back and do that.

I: What kind of errors were there on the paper?

J: Well, like spelling errors. I was trying to type "has," but I was thinking of "save" and I typed "saved."

These students relied on their teachers to help them edit and revise. While their papers might look more correct as a result, students need to be placed in the position of learning the skills themselves. Self-assessment can play a helpful role in this.

In contrast to direct correction, many teachers have adopted the use of rubrics to assess student writing and to engage students in self-assessment (Kuhs, Johnson, Arguso, & Monrad, 2001). Rubrics are scales with three or more levels of performance. Some are *holistic,* with a single response to a piece of student work; *analytic* rubrics include scales on different aspects of student writing. Ideally students and teachers communicate clearly with the explicit expectations put forth in rubrics. In Amelia's experience, when presenting her story and picture of the study of alienation (Figure 3.7, page 37), she described the use of rubrics with five levels of performance, without reference to her teacher.

Amy: Well, we have this system, it's like "novice," "apprentice," "practitioners" and "scholar" and "not yet." Like you didn't show anything. Like that you learned something in the class and then "novice" is like you showed a little bit of it and then "apprentice" is like you showed it but not consistently and "practitioner" is you showed it consistently and then, "scholar," you showed it and you taught to somebody else. So if you score all practitioners you did well and then you can get like a couple of apprentices that means you did pretty well, but scholar is best.

Interviewer: How did you assess yourself on that assignment?

A: I gave myself all "practitioners."

Amelia did not reference her teacher's assessment; for her, and indeed, for many students, self-assessment was more salient. Amelia's experience supports the goals of the use of rubrics. In fact, we were struck overall by the absence in our study of much student commentary about grades and teacher evaluation. To them, engagement was not about earning a grade; it was about personal growth and self-realization, as Amelia made clear.

Writing in the content areas can offer students opportunities for critical thinking, for furthering their learning, and for personal satisfaction. Writing also offers challenge and some struggle. For students to cross into times of intellectual growth, struggle is necessary. Here we suggest ways to help students handle the struggle.

STRATEGIES TO TRY IN YOUR CLASSROOM

Discovery

True learning occurs when students uncover and discover ideas for themselves. The suggestion that educators create opportunities for discovery is not a new recommendation, but it needs to be viewed in terms of the realities of schools. There are difficulties in making these preferences manifest, for creating the contexts for discovery is much more difficult than it is to tell, to lecture, to assign a reading. To design open exploration activities is to open the unknown; the loss of control can be frightening to teachers. And to construct situations for discovery takes a lot more teaching—and planning—time.

Yet when we seriously consider thoughts like Paula's—"Yeah, like every day they would focus on one subject and they would draw stuff on the board . . . and then hand us sheets of paper to do for homework and stuff. I didn't really like it at all"—or Linzzy's—"That's not good to just also have the teacher tell you everything. We do a lot of that. I've always done that with all the teachers"—we confront strong reminders that it is worthwhile to enable students to construct their own knowledge. This is the true meaning of *education*: to "educe" or draw out.

Ron recalled the excitement of a reenactment through which he learned about a key Civil War battle. Reenactment is one of many techniques teachers can use to create opportunities for student discovery. Science experiments, researching and writing biographies and reports, problem solutions, simulations of events, explorations of solutions to a real-world problem, are all ways of student discovery. Discovery projects tend to be long term, but they do not have to be. For example, students might interview an older person and write a brief biography. Finally, physical movement in making posters and models, movement during simulations, and talk during group interaction are all active techniques that, ideally, are part of every school day.

Learning by Teaching

In her coral reef project, Paula liked teaching about the reef through her game and the poster she developed. Teaching others by reading books to younger students, by sharing papers with classmates, by presenting the results of research, and in presenting in panels are a few of the opportunities students have for teaching. A challenge for students, knowing as they do what is boring and what is interesting, is to design their own presentations to truly engage their classmates.

Supporting Discovery

1. *The Context.* Students have said they need a certain kind of environment in which to work. Noise levels that inhibit group work are mentioned often in the data. Ron, for example, pictured the negative effects of disorganization in Chapter 2. The teacher's responsibility is to organize and control movement and noise so that work can be effectively accomplished.

> How does your current classroom layout facilitate discovery?
>
> Hinder discovery?

The furniture should support discovery. For example, moveable desks and tables are conducive to creating small groups, as well as to creating open spaces. Discovery can be noisy, so teachers need to ensure that groups of students who are experimenting have space to do so without disturbing others. Engaging students in the development of ground rules or expectations also helps establish the classroom norms.

2. *Materials.* Discovery classrooms are filled with hands-on materials of all sorts, for hands-on interactions with flora, fauna, minerals, and other exciting, tangible artifacts. In this chapter Charlie speaks of the dullness of a film on the solar system. It was boring, he said, because it was repetitive. Watching video or film without interaction can be far too passive for young people who need to interact. Of course, an exciting video or film that stimulates discussion and further study is common to the active learning classroom. Even less exciting materials can be made engaging with purpose-setting questions, opening links to prior knowledge, and methods for gathering the important information quickly. When researching, students often prefer exploration on the Internet, and if using books, middle schoolers can begin to gather materials from several sources.

Controversy in School

When students learn to speak their minds, listen to different points of view, weigh evidence and reason, and respect others' conclusions, they are learning to participate in a democracy. If young people learn that preference for a point of view or for a candidate is to be kept to themselves, they miss the opportunities to strengthen their thinking by explaining and defending, to anticipate alternative points of view, and to respect other patterns of reasoning. They will depend on those whose thinking is similar. Worse, they may come to believe that all beliefs are private and unchanging. Ultimately, such thinking results in a growing population of disengaged citizens.

One of us has visited a classroom where the sharing of current events is always a key part of every day. Students bring forth information and reactions to political and social matters of all kinds: issues of child abuse by priests, questions of marriage for gay and lesbian persons, analyses of government officials, and the like. There teacher and students share and listen, and all are better informed. Classrooms like this one help students understand the importance of engaging in respectful debate and consideration of issues of importance.

Good classroom discussion is the result of teaching, modeling, and practice. Paula spoke about people yelling in a "discussion" of abortion. At the outset it is really important that ground rules for discussion be established, published, and referenced. Such rules or expectations outline ways to react to one another, listening behaviors, and response behaviors. When they model, teachers often are concerned about bringing in their own views to the classroom. It is true that one must be wary of imposing one's point of view unfairly. But teachers can accept without comment student expressions and help students think critically. If teachers want to share their points of view, it should be done so that other conclusions are possible.

Some teachers deliberately show their students instances where authors of books disagree. This juxtaposition of fact, opinion, and analysis is a positive practice, for it stimulates student research, critical thinking, and understanding the processes of thinking and writing. We want our students to be independent thinkers, so we encourage exploration and construction.

Writing in the Content Areas

There are several ways in which student thinking is enhanced through writing. Logs prompted by teachers that respond to content area learning not only demonstrate thinking but can occur just at those points where links to ideas can be made. For example, after a group of students has presented a panel discussion on the contributions of Martin Luther King, Jr., to the civil rights movement, a teacher prompt to the class might be, "Write down what you think was King's most important contribution. Try to think of another historical figure who also contributed in a similar way." Thus, the prompt encourages the synthesis of one experience with another, a step toward greater critical thinking.

It is not easy to transfer fleeting, new ideas into writing. Many of us have experienced the difficulty of thinking and thinking and finally pulling ideas together, finding the words to express the ideas, and writing and rewriting them. As we go through the process, we learn; we learn as those fleeting ideas take shape and are communicated clearly. It is important for students to learn through writing workshops that their struggles are common ones. Amelia told us that she realized how much she had learned after writing a paper and seeing that there was a lot for her to present.

Variation in Classroom Writing

Our students told us of many kinds of writing. Lively classes are those that allow students to find their writing "voices" by offering occasions for poetry writing, for free writing, for drafting, editing, and rewriting, for writing narrative, for writing reports, for writing scripts for plays, for writing needed in PowerPoint presentations, and so forth.

Using the Computer

Students should be able to spend enough time composing and editing to become familiar with all the editing potential available. We are also cognizant of those writers who continue to be more comfortable composing with pen or pencil. The point is that in the process of learning to write, most of us choose from among the potential processes. Our recommendation that students learn to compose and edit on the computer is to offer that as one possibility as they grow in experience. Further, computers housed in the classroom, or on portable laptop carts, respond to the changing needs of teachers and students with greater versatility than the traditional lab environment.

Fluency

Kevin told us of his lack of writing fluency in his sad remark about how everyone else finished journal writing before he did. To help students whose writing is not fluent, students for whom writing is a particular chore, teachers might consider alternative ways to communicate. Some students may benefit from by-passing hand writing altogether and learning to write on the computer. Others may tape record their ideas to listen to and later write. Free writing can be used, writing that has no "correction." Rather than marking errors in these initial, hopefully more fluent communications, teachers should select one or two areas of focus and then gradually respond to others.

Audience

Writing assignments should always include a consideration of audience. Students should know when they are writing only for themselves, when they are writing to a peer, when they are writing for publishing, when they are writing a first draft for a final report, when they are writing a culminating project, and when they are preparing a piece for their writing portfolio. Gradually, as they discuss and consider the meaning of the different audiences, they reflect and gain perspective on their work. Audience is inextricably linked to purpose, and real purposes and audiences heighten engagement considerably.

Editing

Ultimately, good writers are good editors. Learning to edit one's work takes time and explicit teaching. When students need more challenge, mini-lessons are appropriately presented in the context of current writing.

Because it can be difficult to "see" one's own writing, paired editing can follow mini-lessons. For example, after a mini-lesson on possible ways to organize a report presented visually by the teacher, each person in a pair might examine a draft to think about its organization and do the same for his partner's paper organization. Similarly, after a mini-lesson on the use of the colon, pairs of students can look first at their own and then their partner's drafts for places where colons might be used.

Subsequently, after mini-lessons, the teacher can mark instances where the particular element has been used successfully, thereby reacting to success rather than writing errors. When, however, there is need to support student editing, rather than mark where the error occurs, teachers find it more successful to check in the margin where a change is needed (and not in red ink!). The student is then challenged to find the error and correct it; thus her editing skills are enhanced.

Self-Assessment and Writing

Throughout, the students referenced their own assessment of their performance more than referencing external assessment, even their teachers' evaluations. We noted that was true in writing, as well. Amelia talked about the rubric used at the conclusion of her study of alienation. It was her own response that was remembered. Farnan and Dahl (2003) suggest that analytic rubrics are preferable to holistic. With analytic rubrics, students or teachers assess a piece of writing on several factors (for example, organization, content, punctuation, descriptive language) rather than in an overall assessment. Criteria need to be established for each factor and each level delineated. Commonly, when students are engaged in self-assessments, no more than three or four levels of performance are used.

The greatest value of rubrics is probably how they can encourage student reflection on learning. Teachers often successfully share the rubric at the beginning of a particular study with their students, and, in this way, the criteria and levels are clear. In this way, students know what is expected.

In the inquiry disciplines, how do you . . .

- Honor student questions?
- Engage students actively with materials?
- Foster critical thinking through meaningful debate?
- Utilize writing-to-learn?
- Encourage self-assessment?

CONCLUSION

The students we interviewed shared remarkable insights into their learning. They described rich examples of satisfying inquiry based on their own, relevant questions; active and engaging approaches to Science and Social Studies that included hands-on investigation, debate, and writing. While of course they did not agree with one another about everything, several themes emerged as central to engaging young adolescents effectively. Each student met with us, one on one, in the privacy of safe school space to share these insights. What might happen if students and teachers engaged in this dialogue with one another, in their own classroom space? Would drawing and talk about times of engagement be a viable bridge to enhancing learning and teaching? We describe two teachers who tried just this in the chapter that follows.

7 Consulting *Your* Students

The critical and inspiring insights offered by the students we have worked with have convinced us that educators at all levels have a lot to learn from students. (Shultz & Cook-Sather, 2001, p. xiii)

Who has power in your classroom?
Who makes decisions about what is studied?

The questions in the box on this page may seem like silly questions. For the most part, teachers and other adults at the school, district, state, and federal levels make the decisions. Yet many teachers involve their students in decision making where they can, and the students' messages here suggest that they, too, want to have a say. The students presented in this book reveal the importance of empowering learners with real input into such decisions. Listening to learners can decrease the gap between learner needs and classroom experiences.

While forthcoming in his conversations with us, Charlie was a fourth grader who revealed a reluctance to voice his own learning needs or preferences within his own classroom. For example, when asked if he would ever tell the teacher that he already knew the information contained within a video on the solar system, and that he felt it was boring, he replied, "Probably not." This reluctance to advocate for his own interests was echoed in his later response:

Interviewer: So what would you do if you had a question about space and it wasn't part of the study, would you say or ask anything?

Charlie: No.

Students like Charlie can be easy to have in classrooms; they present few conflicts to management. Yet, they also present the perhaps greater challenge of going unnoticed. How is the teacher to know that Charlie is essentially disengaged, detached, without inviting him to talk about his schooling experience? Eliciting feedback from learners can be difficult: it's hard to make the time; it may be a challenge to hear what students say about one's teaching without a bruised ego; and it's problematic in that inviting the feedback then calls for action. Yet, honoring students in this way can lead to a better fit between student and school. With better fit, engagement is heightened. This chapter shares our experiences working with teachers to incorporate this method into their own work.

> How might you adapt these techniques for your own classroom?

LEARNING FROM LEARNERS

This final chapter turns to the question of how best to engage learners in discussion of their experiences and how that discussion might inform your instruction. We include here comments from middle school teachers who have seen the drawings and heard and read interviews. We describe the use of drawing and talk in groups in two specific classrooms. And we suggest ways you can begin the process in your own classroom, including suggestions for eliciting student perceptions to enhance student engagement in learning.

Discussions With Teachers

In talking with teachers at in-service meetings, at regional and national conferences, and in private conversations, we have been struck by teachers' favorable reaction to the role learners can play in informing instruction. Teachers have liked the idea that pedagogy can be adapted so that students feel a greater degree of comfort and fit with school. "It is helpful to be reminded that our students can offer us a hand in designing lessons. They can tell us a lot if we ask them," said one. Others told us they intended to use the process in their classrooms. "I was really fascinated by the drawings. I had never thought to ask students to reflect on what experiences they have had that were meaningful, or not engaging. I intend to try it." And the use of drawing, in particular, to elicit student perspective was powerful for some: "Looking at the children's drawings gave me an entirely new way of

> Is the use of drawing and talk an end in itself?

viewing what they find interesting and engaging." Whether from rural, suburban, or urban schools, these middle school teachers responded to the process of drawing and talk favorably.

What might happen if you talked with your own students?

INTO CLASSROOMS

Throughout our initial project, when soliciting drawing and talk from individuals around times of engagement and disengagement, we wondered how groups of students might respond to similar requests by their own teachers. Would the same kinds of issues emerge? Would students be willing to share through drawing and talk? Two skilled sixth grade teachers agreed to use drawing and talk with their own students as a way to explore and improve their practice. As before, we obtained permission from students, parents, and administrators prior to beginning this stage of our work. The two teachers, and we, were heartened by the willingness of their students and the powerful insights they provided.

JEN'S CLASSROOM

Jen teaches sixth grade Science and Language Arts at Crosstown School, a K–8 school that serves a town in the ski country of southern Vermont. (The twenty-one students in Jen's class exchange classes with another sixth grade class and teacher.) Jen emphasizes equally the values of class as community and of student intellectual growth in her teaching.

Once the students were asked to draw a time of engagement (see outline of process in "And Now, *Your* Classroom" on page 123), they asked a few questions about the drawing task, but quickly turned to work seriously at the task. They finished in about 30 minutes. Jen then invited the students in turn to present their pictures. She assured them all that sharing their pictures was optional, but only two students chose not to share their pictures. She asked the students to explain why their chosen time was engaging, and they did, enthusiastically. Altogether, with the drawing and the discussion, the activity took about 70 minutes.

About Math

In several respects the process reinforced what the students in the first stage of our study portrayed. For example, Math as a measure of ability emerged again. Five of the Crosstown students chose to depict a time in

Figure 7.1	Archer's Picture of Math Class	Figure 7.2	Alice's Picture of Math

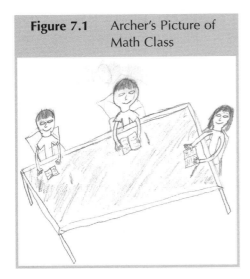

Math as engaging. Two of them illustrated a moment from the previous year when they, and another student, were in a challenging, exciting Math class. These students demonstrated considerable confidence in their Math ability. We turn first to Archer's picture that portrays the experience of the confident Math students (Figure 7.1). He showed the students in the special, more advanced Math class with their paper and pencils at hand, each smiling.

Archer explained, "Mine is last year. We were in this Algebra class in the library by ourselves. Because Math was like boring for us so Ms. S put us in this class. . . . And it was like really challenging and fun. Because like when there is challenge, you think harder. So it's more fun."

His classmate, Frieda, the girl on the right in Archer's picture, agreed: "When I was in the little Algebra group instead of doing the regular Math, it was a lot more fun and a lot more interesting. I like to do it. Because . . . we had harder math. It was new and I caught on quick." She wrote on the back of her picture, "I wish we could do it again. [I] liked having control over what we did." These two students reminded us of Brian, who was featured in Chapter 4. Like them, Brian had focused on a previous time when he had enjoyed challenging Math.

In contrast, "more fun," "more interesting," and "control over what we did" were not characteristics of Math from the other three students, represented here with a picture by Alice (Figure 7.2). They had a very different take on their Math ability. "I'm not good at Math," said one; "I didn't really get it and I'm not really good at Math," said others. Alice showed exactly what it was that she finally understood; from the bubble, "The denominators have to be the same in order to add." She demonstrated this concept in the drawing.

"I felt really good about it because I actually understood it." We asked what helped. "Well, he went step by step." Alice's talk and her classmates' was much like Georgia's in Chapter 4: Step-by-step progression through processes was helpful and engaging.

Jen, their teacher, responded to this idea of Math as the measure: "I was surprised by those who are poor in Math, that they shared so freely" in the group situation. The drawing and talk experience made it possible for the students to feel safe so they could share their feelings.

Active Learning

Active approaches to learning were also central to Jen's sixth graders, like the individual students featured in Chapter 3. For example, three girls focused on "cookie mining" as a time of deep engagement. One wrote on the back of her picture, "It was fun because we got to do our own mining corporation. It was like a mini ground mining. If your equipment [tooth-picks] broke, you had to pay for it. We had to dig up the chocolate chips as our rock. The cookie is the ground." Jen asked her students more about the role of action and involvement in learning. They responded, "Well, some people like hands-on." And, "Some people like to do things that are excit-ing." And, "A lot of people like to do new things and challenge."

Competing

Jen listened to the students' sharing of the mining activity and added, "A lot of you who did [choose cookie mining] did because it was hands-on. How many would choose it because it was almost like a competition? It was a real challenge to see if you could make money." Most hands went up. Arlene's picture (Figure 7.3) showed the competitive element. She rep-resented these two pairs of students happily and eagerly offering to share their findings.

AND Working Together

Jen's students also revealed the impact of the combination of action and cooperative work on their engagement. We include two relevant pic-tures, Charles's and Carter's.

Charles stood up eagerly when it was his time to share his picture. With enthusiasm, he explained about his drawing (Figure 7.4):

"And it was a group. And we made a house. We made people. And I think David was in my group and we made this huge house even though we were only blacksmiths. We made a mansion. We had a workshop.

Figure 7.3   Arlene's Picture of Cookie Mining

Figure 7.4   Charles's Time of Engagement

Figure 7.5   Carter's Group Activity

A kitchen. And I think we had a barn in the back for like pigs and stuff. And um I like it because I was involved."

We don't need Carter's words to show that his engaging time also involved fun working together (Figure 7.5). These boys all seem to be involved with something in boxes.

"I did it from last year. Erosion deposition. We had this little dam thing. With like water and stuff. I thought it was like fun because it was like hands-on. And we got to like build a little dam of Popsicle sticks. . . . We had these little bins. We had like cups. We poured water in the cups. And washed away the dirt. We had a house below the dam, near the water, and it got washed away."

Clearly these young adolescents liked working together to solve problems. As one girl wrote on the back of her picture, "We all got a lot done because we helped each other. This taught me that if you work together you can get a lot done."

Topical Interest

The topic under study was what engaged several students. When they could choose their topic, two boys drew about their class study of Egypt;

another chose the Revolutionary War and depicted his teacher writing information on the board for the students. The students were currently involved in researching a personal interest, and there emerged drawings of fish, a computer screen with information about trebuchet, medieval weaponry, information about hunting, and reading about Dian Fossey.

Jen pursued this idea that personal interest played in engagement. "How many of you chose because of subject?" About half of the group agreed, and of those, when Jen asked if they were already interested, only a couple of hands went down. Jen observed, "So almost everybody chose a subject they were already interested in."

Jen's Learnings

After we spent time in Jen's class, we talked with her. The idea of honoring students by asking them when and how they were engaged was significant. She felt that the students "liked that their ideas were important. They like thinking like being valued and listened to."

Jen also found that drawing was critical to the activity: "Drawing themselves in the situations. It's something they can relate to. It doesn't have same block [as just talk]. They might be afraid. They are drawing—and learning about who they are." Jen added a thought about drawing and talk, noting too its potential impact on teachers. "It would be good for a new teacher. Here's an activity for kids to do—not just what the kids are learning, but learning about learning helps. They learn to understand their preferences."

Jen observed the potential for both teachers' and students' growth as a result of listening to learners. At the same time, she acknowledged the demands of the regular curriculum and commented on how difficult it is for her even to include all the Science inquiry she wants. It is a challenge to find the time for exploring student perceptions through drawing; still, the activity in Jen's room produced work that validated some of the earlier themes, especially about Math and active learning. Also important, it also provided new reference points for Jen to use to encourage her student's reflections on their learning. And it created an opportunity for Jen to follow her own line of professional inquiry through dialogue with students.

> How do you reflect on and modify your own teaching?

KATHY'S CLASSROOM

Kathy teaches sixth grade at the Southaven Village School in a very small, rural village where students study together for all their K–6 years. Like

Jen, Kathy is a serious teacher with a comfortable management style. Strong curriculum is evident; Kathy is concerned with her students' growth and development in both academic and social spheres.

We had two drawing experiences in Kathy's class of seventeen students, several months apart. The first occasion was for drawing and talk activities about a time of engagement. In this instance, after the prompt, questions and clarifying answers, and the drawing task itself, students first described their pictures to their neighbors and thereby prepared for the group sharing. Each drawing was shown to the group as the student told the story. In this instance we tried to encourage student interaction over the pictures and stories. We conducted the conversation while Kathy noted what was said on the board; the activity took 55 minutes.

Active Learning—Again

Active learning again emerged as important to engaging middle schoolers. For example, four boys drew pictures of a reenactment of the 1748 Trout Battle between English/colonial soldiers and Native Americans that occurred on a river near the school (Figure 7.6 presents one student's drawing). Kathy wrote on the board as these four students described that experience and their drawings:

Made props and clothing.

Side projects were fun.

We learned history.

I liked going down to the river and engaging the enemy.

One of the boys said, "We were only supposed to kill six of them but we ended up killing all of them." To him, this became quite real. "This massacre happened right down here on the river."

Interests and Preferences

Perhaps because these students had been in school together for many years, they felt safe to share some deeply held personal preferences that seemed to serve as a bridge to engagement. We present here two of these more unusual depictions.

Danielle has 10 horses; her own, Lucky, is on the right (Figure 7.7). She used words in the drawing to explain that they were "studying countries through horses," and on the day depicted, in third grade, they were learning about Arabians and Arabia. We noted that the students were all girls.

Figure 7.6 John's Drawing of the Massacre Reenactment

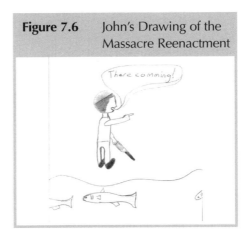

Figure 7.7 Danielle's Love of Her Horse

Figure 7.8 Roberta's Need for Privacy

As Danielle said, "Lots of girls in our class loved horses." Her teacher certainly drew on their interest that year when teaching Geography.

Roberta explained, "I was home-schooled. And this was about three years ago. I was reading in my Social Studies book. It really sparked my interest and I was like . . . *Oh!* It was about . . . how women liked to sneak into some wars. Like in the Revolutionary War . . . It helped me to be alone, to have a time of silence. I locked myself into my room. And I also . . . on purpose because I had the key. One of those old houses that you had skeleton keys to get in and out . . . and you could get out of to a roof. So I kind of went outside to think a little while and came back in to read some more."

Roberta showed some of the outside in the window (Figure 7.8). The carefully drawn perspective on the ceiling put Roberta back in the room, the student with her book before her and books at her side. Alone and studious, Roberta remarked on the accomplishment of reading "like five chapters that day." Roberta's reference back to when she was home-schooled was poignant, given her circumstance of being in school with others close around her.

Kathy could find in these drawings and talk material for increasing her students' feeling of fit with school. Bringing horses into Danielle's studies is an obvious response, but so might be attempts to extend Danielle's interests outward. With Roberta, a private talk about her need for quiet and solitude might result in the opportunity to read and study in some quiet corner of the school, when needed.

A Special Case

Nat's picture (Figure 7.9) was really unusual when compared with all the pictures we have collected from young adolescents.

Nat explained, "This is me reading a book, and I'm in the nightmare land with yoga" (from Weis & Hickman, 2003). Nat represented how, as he took on his character, he traveled within the book. His is a representation of the feelings and meaning of the book to him rather than the more conventional representation of himself reading. "I put myself in the main character's shoes. He's my favorite character. I think he's really cool. He rescues and everything. So I put myself in his shoes and what he would do in that situation. What he was doing I would want him to do."

We thought Nat's time of engagement in the midst of this book quite wonderful in its ability to communicate to others the essence of his total engagement, his total identification with this favorite character. The other students, too, were also intrigued by his presenting himself right in the middle of the story. The illustration of self inside a book might be an opportunity for others to try, for other ways of sharing a book experience with classmates.

Figure 7.9 Inside Nat's Book

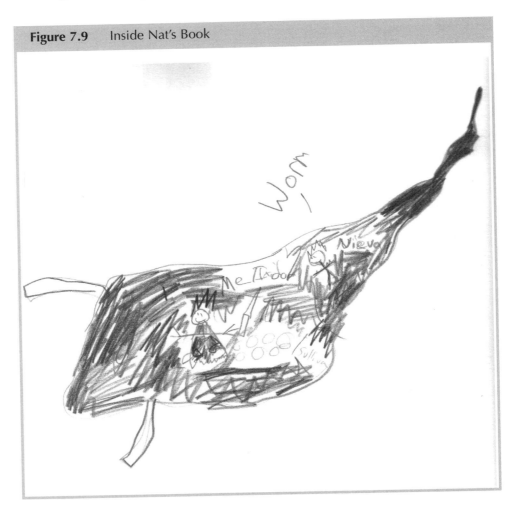

Kathy's Learnings

Kathy responded in writing to the experience. One powerful reaction pertained to Math. Fred had chosen to draw a picture about Math and had said, "We did a portfolio problem and it was easy for me to concentrate. We had already had one like so I knew how to do it. . . . I reflected on it. That it looked like another problem we did so I knew how to do it."

Kathy was surprised by Fred's direct analysis of his success in the Math Portfolio class. "The biggest part that stands out to me is the piece that involves Fred and what he said about Math. Math is not an easy subject for Fred. He often gets lost and struggles. Also, he usually doesn't verbalize his needs. It really surprised me how forthcoming he was. I was also encouraged by his comment about recognizing and connecting his Math experiences. It was a validation of my teaching practices!" Fred was able to complete the problem successfully because of familiarity, because of his ability to make connections and to build on previous learning. Kathy may be able to help him associate new problems with old ones now they have both learned from his successful experience.

Even though this was a small group and she had taught some of the students in the previous year, the exercise led Kathy to even greater understanding of her students and their needs:

"I learned some new things about students who I have for the first time this year. Who likes to take a test, who likes to have more time to do things, who reads for enjoyment, and so on and so forth. I also learned more about the students I had last year for fifth grade. Their comments showed maturity and growth from last year. I like that! This exercise was another reminder to me how important differentiated instruction is to effective teaching. The students who participated in the Trout Battle reenactment remembered how great it was to 'live' the history of their town. . . . The students' comments made me realize even more about how enthusiasm is so important."

In a sense, Kathy viewed students' times of engagement as an assessment of her teaching. She could use the information to assess what

> What would your students identify as engaging? As disengaging?

they found engaging in her class. Certainly, there is great potential for feedback about what is engaging when taking drawing and talk into classrooms.

Beyond Engagement

For the next drawing and talk activity several months later, when we asked Kathy if she wanted to do the exercise again and this time with her own prompt, she said she wanted to examine students' social experiences, how students support each other, or not. We planned for Kathy to conduct the questioning, and we would take notes. After careful consideration about how to word the prompt, Kathy asked them to "Think of a time in school when you felt most comfortable. Maybe you were alone; maybe you were in a group. It could be this year, another year. This was a time when you felt at ease, good." They were asked not to look at others' drawings so they could concentrate on personal experience. In this case, the students spent 30 minutes drawing and 17 minutes talking.

There were a wide variety of responses to this prompt. Several students drew pictures of times when working or playing with friends. Several agreed with Fred, who said, "I like it [recess] because you can forget about everything and just have fun." Matt also expressed this relief from pressure, but he showed himself staying in, with a friend, just talking. Matt depicted two boys, from the back, standing in class. They

Figure 7.10 When Cate Felt Comfortable

Figure 7.11 Teddy at the End of the Year

appeared relaxed, as Matt said, "This is snack time. Free Time. I don't have to worry about work. I don't have to go out in the cold and maybe get stuck. I'm just comfortable." Cate recalled a time from a couple of years before. Like Matt, Cate showed herself with a friend (Figure 7.10). "It was recess. We jumped rope the whole time. I felt comfortable because I was with a friend I was close to."

Several students depicted times when they were alone. Teddy's drawing (Figure 7.11) was interesting, as it spoke to a time of reflection and change. Teddy explained, "This was last year after graduation. Everyone had left. Me and my mom stayed to clean up. My brother and me went out to play on the playground. After a while I came back to help my mom clean. This is me looking back at the playground. Normally it's noisy. But it was nice and quiet and I could think about it and the others."

This second visit with Kathy's class took us beyond the issue of engagement and offered opportunities for reflections into other aspects of school life. The variety of representation of "comfort" suggested that drawing and talk are flexible tools for opening discussion for many aspects of school life. When drawing a specific time, with details of that moment included, students put themselves back into a concrete moment. As they think about their experiences, and when they listen to their classmates, middle schoolers are able to move into more abstract, more wide ranging thinking about how they learn. The outcome is more information for teachers, feelings of shared responsibility, and, important for the students, greater knowledge of how they learn.

We were heartened by the experiences in these classrooms. The teachers invited their students into the conversation; they let students know their opinions were valued, and in return the students offered insightful perspectives on schooling. Empowering students with input into teaching and learning approaches gives teachers another mechanism for reflective practice, for adding to their repertoires another means for examining systematically their pedagogy and making changes based on that reflection.

AND NOW *YOUR* CLASSROOM

Here we include specific suggestions for initiating drawing and talk activities in classrooms. While the suggestions emerge from our experiences with the method, they clearly are not written in stone. We urge teachers to experiment with and explore the technique. We believe teachers should base the prompts on their own authen-

> What do you want to learn from your own students?

tic questions about their professional practice and their students' learning. We do, however, suggest that the initial prompt be of a time of engagement, as teachers have found it to be a fruitful starting place. To begin this way accentuates the positive as a starting point for potentially more difficult conversations and sets a climate for future work.

Preparation

• Purpose. To open dialogue and create a way for students to focus in on a time of engagement. What do you hope to learn from your students? What area(s) of your curriculum or practice would benefit from their input?

• Schedule. Plan for a minimum of 50 minutes or more several weeks into the school year.

• Materials. Students enjoy having a choice of pencils, colored pencils, crayons, and markers for their drawing.

> Have I . . .
>
> ☐ Identified what I want to learn from my students?
> ☐ Found a 50-minute block of time we can devote to this work?
> ☐ Compiled enough paper, colored pencils, crayons, and markers for the group?
> ☐ Found or borrowed a tape recorder for the conversation?
> ☐ Tested the tape recorder with a tape and batteries or outlet?

They also note the drawings are valued when given heavy drawing paper. We strongly recommend the use of a tape recorder in order to learn more exactly what your students are experiencing. Some students may be distracted by the recorder at the start of the activity. Telling them you understand this and that they have three minutes to goof around with it but then must move on can be a helpful way to let them clown with a clear end in sight. We have found students quickly lose their concern and become accustomed to its presence in the classroom.

Implementation

1. The Prompt

"This drawing activity is a bit different from what we've done. For this drawing, think of a time when you were really learning, when you felt focused and successful. Think of that time in school; imagine the room, the people, the materials and draw that particular time. Put in the details. Don't worry about the drawing—there is no good or bad drawing—it is just a representation of your experience."

When teachers are introducing the activity, students sometimes are puzzled. It is important to give the prompts with authority and simplicity. Expand on the idea of a time when they felt good, perhaps when they succeeded, when they knew they were learning. Help them focus by advising them to pay no attention to others' drawings until after everyone is finished.

As demonstrated with Kathy, you later may want to explore student experiences in other aspects of school life. For example, you may wish to focus on one subject; or perhaps the social experience of school is what would be profitable. Maybe there is one time of day that you are particularly struggling with. We strongly recommend creative exploration; there are few limits to the possibilities of this strategy for enhancing student-centered teaching.

2. The Drawing Activity

During the time the students are drawing, it helps to encourage them in your usual ways. You may want to circulate freely in the room, making sure all students have equal access to the materials, and encouraging them to remember that "it's not about the art" but rather about their ideas. If the group is fairly independent, it can be powerful to engage in your own drawing, and share it with the class as a fellow learner.

Students' Frequently Asked Questions

(with answers!):

Q: Should it be this year?
A: Any year.
Q: Can it be any subject?
A: Yes.
Q: Does it have to be in school?
A: Yes.
Q: Can I put in words?
A: Yes.

3. Sharing With Neighbor

If you include this part, give each pair a few minutes. The drawings the students have completed are of very personal, individual moments of satisfactory learning. The first step in moving from the particular to larger instances of engagement occurs well when the sharing occurs in a relatively private conversation with another student. As one shares one's experience, and the neighbor asks questions and shows interest, the student begins to look at his or her drawing and think about the experience with more perspective. This piece, sharing with the neighbor, is very helpful; it is not absolutely essential, as shown in Jen's class where we did not have enough time.

4. Sharing in Whole Group

The students each show their pictures. Sometimes it helps for you (or one of the students) to take the pictures around for all to see while the student is talking. Choose either to go around round robin fashion or to ask for volunteer responses. We strongly recommend that those who feel uncomfortable about sharing not be required to do so. Typically, however, almost all will share when the exercise occurs in the context of trust. Start the process by reminding students of the need to show interest and respect for others. We have found it helpful to move back and forth between comments and questions to the individuals presenting and comments and questions to the group to encourage reflection.

This is a necessary part of the process, and you will be busy listening to each student while also focusing the group's attention. With larger classes, students might meet as smaller groups to share their drawings. The groups then can be charged to summarize the themes emerging from their groups for the whole class.

We have found that questions to the whole group can help the process. For example:

"James is saying that he needs careful, step-by-step directions. Is that true for anyone else?"

"Emma appreciates group work when I have assigned students particular roles. Do you agree with that or do you prefer deciding on your own?"

"Do you see here in Susan's picture how she showed her preference for quiet?"

"How has Mason shown in the drawing how much he liked the simulation?"

"Do you see a pattern emerging?"

Questions like these for a few moments take the conversation toward the larger picture of student experience. It is also very helpful to ask the students what questions or comments they might have about another's experience.

5. Summarize

At the conclusion of the sharing, ask the students to consider what they have learned about their own and their classmates' learning. Share what you have learned. Ask the students what they think of the exercise. Gather the drawings for later reflection.

Reflections

• *Notes.* Write down your impressions of the exercise as soon afterward as possible.

• *Further Reflections.* When you can, sit with the pictures and tape. Jot down each student's main points and what is represented in the picture. When completed, look over these further notes and the initial notes to explore the themes that have emerged as well as individual needs that appear. Listening to the tapes and looking at the drawings takes time, a commodity in short supply in busy teachers' schedules, but we urge that this be part of the process for students say important things quickly and quietly. It is not always possible to remember everything, and themes emerge on reflection. Look at the drawings while listening to the tape and jotting down important points. Perhaps you will find similar themes as those that repeat themselves here: preferences for active learning, the value of choice, the influence of the constant presence of others, differences in responses to different subjects, Math performance as definition, and so forth. It is likely you will learn about individuals to support your work with them; you might learn of the student who needs quiet, the person who can perform better when he or she is helped to create links with prior experience.

Following Through

• *Talking With Students.* When comfortable, spend a couple of moments sharing with the class what you are learning.

• *Adapting to Feedback.* Where reasonable, shift practice toward student feedback. Be sure to be explicit when you are responding to their feedback and thus are honoring them. The payoff will be great! Every time you make a change in response to student drawing and talk, and you tell your students you are doing so, you increase the students' sense of power, their experience of fit with school, the likelihood of their engagement in learning. When it is not possible to adapt, it is important to explain why. And, when different students demonstrate preferences for different modes of learning—for group or individual work, for example—discuss possible solutions together. The students feel honored; you will, too.

Reflecting on Learners' Drawings

1. *Be guided by your question.* Keep your question in mind as you interpret the images. Ask how the whole collection and how each drawing addresses your question. How do they contribute to an increased understanding of your topic?

2. *Keep track of your reactions and ideas in a journal or log.* We know teachers are incredibly busy, but sometimes an idea that seems silly or irrelevant early on becomes useful again later. We always think we are going to remember our keen insights or inspirations, but unless you write them down or draw them, you risk forgetting them.

3. *Have students label everything carefully,* so that you can play with images and rearrange them without worrying about being able to identify where they came from, what they are and so forth.

4. *Lay out the data.* You might want to lay them out in different ways, constructing different "wholes" or groupings. There are many ways to "lay out" your data: in columns, circles, or other patterns; on a vertical surface (perhaps taped to the wall) or on a large table. Experiment! It's hard to know what will stand out within a new arrangement unless you try it. Even just moving images around within the same row or framework can unexpectedly throw into relief a feature of the image you place it next to.

5. *Project the data.* One of the most powerful ways we have examined drawings is by making transparencies of the drawings and projecting them onto the wall using overhead projectors. Those with access to more advanced technology can scan the drawings and project the digital images with an LCD projector. Seeing the drawings on a larger scale reveals items in relation to one another, captures another level of emotion of the students, and shows use of white space.

6. *Collaborate.* Each time we have shared students' drawings at national conferences, teachers have pointed out aspects of the images we had not previously noticed or considered. Invite teammates or other colleagues to join you in examining the data. For this work, the more eyes the better!

SOURCE: Adapted from Weber (n.d.), *Analysing Visual Qualitative Data*, Concordia University.

ON LISTENING TO LEARNERS

> Reflecting on the duty I have as a teacher to respect the dignity, autonomy and identity of the student, all of which are in the process of becoming, I ought to think also about how I can develop an educational practice in which that respect, which I know I owe to the student, can come to fruition instead of being simply neglected and denied. Such an educational practice will demand of me permanent critical vigilance in regard to the students. (Friere, 1998, pp. 62–63)

We respect students through our listening and our subsequent action. The students to whom we "listened," both through drawing and talk, expressed clear and poignant insights into the culture of schooling and the complexities of their own learning processes. They led us to understand the crucial role learners might play in constructing and reconstructing the educational system. Their perspectives can improve educational practice, inform educational reform initiatives, and highlight the need for new reform efforts to be undertaken. Cook-Sather (2002) urged us to engage in listening to learners as an ongoing process: "It is the collective student voice, constituted by the many situated, partial, individual voices, that we are missing" (p. 12). We access the collective voice when we "authorize" students' perspectives; when we grant these perspectives both voice and authority; when we invite students to speak and we in turn listen.

References

Allen-Malley, M. G., & Bishop, P. (2000). The power of partners: Two teacher teams. *Schools in the Middle* (pp. 26–30). Reston, VA: National Association of Secondary School Principals.

Alvermann, D. (2002). Effective literacy instruction for adolescents. *Journal of Literacy Research, 34*(2), 189–208.

Andrus, E. (1996). Service learning: Taking students beyond community service. *Middle School Journal, 28*(2), 10–18.

Apple, M., & Beane, J. (Eds.). (1995). *Democratic schools*. Alexandria, VA: Association for Supervision and Curriculum Development.

Arhar, J., & Kromrey, J. (1995). Interdisciplinary teaming and the demographics of membership: A comparison of student belonging in high SES and low SES middle-level schools. *Research in Middle Level Education, 18*(2), 71–88.

Arhar, J. M. (1994). Personalizing the social organization of middle-level school: Does interdisciplinary teaming make a difference? In K. B. Borman & N. P. Greenman (Eds.), *Changing American education: Recapturing the past or inventing the future?* (pp. 325–350). Albany: SUNY Press.

Atwell, N. (Ed.). (1990). *Coming to know: Writing to learn in the intermediate grades*. Portsmouth, NH: Heinemann.

Beane, J. (1993). *A middle school curriculum: From rhetoric to reality* (2nd ed.). Columbus, OH: National Middle School Association.

Beane, J. (1997). *Curriculum integration: Designing the core of democratic education*. New York: Teachers College Press.

Beane, J. A., & Lipka, R. P. (1980). Self-concept and self-esteem: A construct differentiation. *Child Study Journal, 10*(1), 1–6.

Beck, M., & Malley, J. (1998). A pedagogy of belonging. *Reclaiming Children and Youth: Journal of Emotional and Behavioral Problems, 7*(3), 133–137.

Bishop, P., & Pflaum, S. (2005). Middle school students' perceptions of social dimensions as influencers of academic engagement. *Research in Middle Level Education Online, 29*(1).

Bishop, P., & Pflaum, S. (2005). Student perceptions of action, relevance and pace. *Middle School Journal, 36*(4), 4–12.

Bishop, P., & Stevenson, C. (2000). When smaller is greater: Two or three person partner teams. *Middle School Journal, 31*(3), 12–17.

Blachowicz, C., & Ogle, D. (2001). *Reading comprehension: Strategies for independent learners*. New York: Guilford.

Boyer, S., & Bishop, P. (2004). Young adolescent voices: Students' perceptions of interdisciplinary teaming. *Research in Middle Level Education Online, 28*(1).

Bryk, A. S., & Schneider, B. (2002). *Trust in schools: A core resource for improvement.* New York: Russell Sage.

Carnegie Corporation. (1995). *Great transitions: Preparing adolescents for a new century.* Waldorf, MD: Author.

Carnegie Council on Adolescent Development. (1989). *Turning points: Preparing youth for the 21st century.* New York: Carnegie Corporation.

Chard, N. (1990). How learning logs change teaching. In N. Atwell (Ed.), *Coming to know: Writing to learn in the intermediate grades.* Portsmouth, NH: Heinemann.

Charney, R. S. (1992). *Teaching children to care.* Greenfield, MA: Northeast Foundation for Children.

Clasen, D. R. (1987, April 23–26). *Comparisons of rejected, neglected and popular adolescents on psycho-social and cognitive variables.* Paper presented at the Biennial Meeting of the Society for Research in Child Development, Baltimore, MD.

Clinton, P. (2002). The crisis you don't know about. *The Literacy Warriors' Book* (September/October), L4–L15.

Cohen, E. G., & Lotan, R. A. (Eds.). (1997). *Working for equity in heterogeneous classrooms: Sociological theory in practice.* Sociology of Education Series. New York: Teachers College Press.

Collins, P. J. (1990). Bridging the gap. In N. Atwell (Ed.), *Coming to know: Writing to learn in the intermediate grades.* Portsmouth, NH: Heinemann.

Conrad, D., & Hedin, D. (1991). School-based community service: What we know from research and theory. *Phi Delta Kappan, 72*(10), 743–749.

Cook-Sather, A. (2002). Authorizing students' perspectives: Toward trust, dialogue and change in education. *Educational Researcher, 31*(4), 3–14.

Cotton, K. (2001). *Close-Up #7: Expectations and student outcomes.* NorthWest Regional Education Laboratory. Available at http://www.nel.org/scpd/sirs/4/cu7.html

Dewey, J. (1899). School and society. In M. S. Dworkin, *Dewey on education* (pp. 33–90). New York: Teachers College Press.

Dickinson, T., & Erb, T. (1997). *We gain more than we give: Teaming in middle schools.* Columbus, OH: National Middle School Association.

Dreher, M. J. (2000). Fostering reading for learning. In L. Baker, M. J. Dreher, & J. T. Guthrie (Eds.), *Engaging young readers: Promoting achievement and motivation.* New York: Guilford.

Duckworth, E. (1996). *"The having of wonderful ideas" and other essays on teaching and learning.* New York: Teachers College Press.

Duckworth, E. (2001). *Tell me more: Listening to learners explain.* New York: Teachers College Press.

Education Week. (2004, September 29). High tech divide. Available at http://www.edweek.org/ew/articles/2004/09/29/05tech-2.h24.html

Elkind, D. (1984). *All grown up and no place to go: Teenagers in crisis.* New York: Addison-Wesley.

Erickson, F., & Schultz, J. (1992). Students' experience of the curriculum. In P. Jackson (Ed.), *Handbook of research on curriculum* (pp. 465–485). New York: MacMillan.

Farnan, N., & Dahl, K. (2003). Children's writing: Research and practice. In J. Flood, D. Lapp, J. R. Squire, & J. M. Jensen (Eds.), *Handbook of research on teaching the English language arts* (2nd ed.). Mahwah, NJ: Lawrence Erlbaum Associates.

Farner, C. D. (1996). Discipline alternatives: Mending the broken circle. *Learning, 25*(1), 27–29.

Finn, J. D., Pannozzo, G. M., & Achilles, C. M. (2003). The why's of class size: Student behavior in small classes. *Review of Educational Research, 3*(73), 321–368.

Friere, P. (1998). *Pedagogy of freedom: Ethics, democracy and civic courage.* Lanham, MD: Rowman & Littlefield.

Gardner, H. (1993). *Frames of mind* (2nd ed.). New York: Basic Books.

George, P. S., & Stevenson, C. (1988). *Highly effective interdisciplinary teams: Perceptions of exemplary middle school principals.* (ERIC Reproduction Services Document No. ED303866)

Glasser, W. (1986). *Control theory in the classroom.* New York: Harper & Row.

Goodlad, J. L. (1984). *A place called school: Prospects for the future.* New York: McGraw-Hill.

Grannis, J. (1967). The school as a model of society. *Harvard Graduate School of Education Association Bulletin, 12,* 14–27.

Grannis, J. (1978). Task engagement and the consistency of pedagogical controls: An ecological study of differently structured classroom settings. Joint decision-making. *Curriculum Inquiry, 8,* 3–36.

Guthrie, J. T., & Alvermann, D. E. (Eds.). (1999). *Engaged reading: Processes, practices and policy implications.* New York: Teachers College Press.

Guthrie, J. T., & Anderson, E. (1999). Engagement in reading: Processes of motivated, strategic, knowledgeable, social readers. In J. T. Guthrie & D. E. Alvermann (Eds.), *Engaged reading: Processes, practices and policy implications.* New York: Teachers College Press.

Guthrie, J. T., Van Meter, P., McCann, A. D., Wigfield, A., Bennett, L., Poundstone, C. C., Rice, M. E., Faibisch, F. M., Hunt, B., & Mitchell, A. M. (1996). Growth of literacy engagement: Changes in motivations and strategies during concept-oriented reading instruction. *Reading Research Quarterly, 31*(3), 306–332.

Guthrie, J. T., & Wigfield, A. (Eds.). (1997). *Reading engagement: Motivating readers through integrated instruction.* Newark, DE: International Reading Association.

Haney, W., Russell, M., & Bebell, D. (2004, Fall). Drawing on education: Using drawings to document schooling and support change. *Harvard Education Review,* 241–272.

Haney, W., Russell, M., & Jackson, L. (1998). Drawing on education: Using drawings to study and change education and schooling. Grant Proposal submitted to the Spencer Foundation. Boston: Authors.

Harwood, A. M., & Hahn, C. L. (1990). *Controversial issues in the classroom* (ERIC Document Reproduction Service No. ED327453). Available at http://www.ericdigests.org/pre-9218/issues.htm

Hillocks, G. (1986). *Research on written composition: New directions for teachers.* Urbana, IL: ERIC Clearinghouse for Reading and Writing.

Hoyles, C. (1982). The pupil's view of mathematics learning. *Educational Studies in Mathematics, 13*(4), 349–372.

Hoyt, L. (1999). *Revisit, reflect, retell: Strategies for improving reading comprehension.* Portsmouth, NH: Heinemann.

Ivey, G. (2003). "The teacher makes it more explainable" and other reasons to read aloud in the intermediate grades. *The Reading Teacher, 56*(8), 812–814.

Ivey, G., & Broaddus, K. (2001). "Just plain reading": A survey of what makes students want to read in middle school classrooms. *Reading Research Quarterly, 36*(4), 350–377.

Jackson, R., & Davis, G. (2000). *Turning points 2000.* New York & Westerville, OH: Teachers College Press & National Middle School Association.

Johnson, H. L., Pflaum, S., Sherman, E., Taylor, P., & Poole, P. (1996). Focus on teenage parents: Using children's literature to strengthen teenage literacy. *Journal of Adolescent & Adult Literacy, 39*(4), 290–296.

Johnson, R. W., & Johnson, R. T. (1998). *Learning together and alone: Cooperative, competitive and individualistic learning* (3rd ed.). Boston: Allyn & Bacon.

Keene, E. O., & Zimmermann, S. (1997). *Mosaic of thought: Teaching comprehension in a reader's workshop.* Portsmouth, NH: Heinemann.

Knowles, T., & Brown, D. (2000). *What every middle school teacher should know.* Portsmouth, NH: Heinemann.

Kohn, A. (1993). Choices for children: Why and how to let students decide. *Phi Delta Kappan, 75*(1), 8–16, 18–21.

Kridel, C. (1998). Implications for initiating educational change. In R. Lipka, J. Lounsbury, C. Toepfer, G. Vars, S. Allessi, & C. Kridel (Eds.), *The Eight Year Study revisited: Lessons from the past for the present* (pp. 17–56). Columbus, OH: National Middle School Association.

Kuhs, T. M., Johnson, R. L., Arguso, S. A., & Monrad, D. M. (2001). *Put to the test: Tools and techniques for classroom assessment.* Portsmouth, NH: Heinemann.

Kurth, B. (1995). Learning through giving: Using service learning as the foundation for a middle school advisory program. *Middle School Journal, 27*(1), 35–41.

Lee, O., & Anderson, C. W. (1993). Task engagement and conceptual change in middle school science classrooms. *American Educational Research Journal, 30*(3), 585–610.

Lee, V. E., & Loeb, S. (2000). School size in Chicago elementary schools: Effects on teachers' attitudes and students' achievement. *American Educational Research Journal, 37*(1), 3–31.

Lee, V. E., & Smith, J. B. (1993). Effects of school restructuring on the achievement and engagement of middle-grades students. *Sociology of Education, 66,* 164–187.

Levine, M. (2002). *A mind at a time.* New York: Simon & Schuster.

Lin, C-H. (2002). *Literature circles* (ERIC Document Reproduction Service No. ED469925). Available at http://www.ericdigests.org/2003-3/circles.htm

Loewen, J. W. (1996). *Lies my teacher told me: Everything your American history textbook got wrong.* New York: New Press.

Maerhoff, G. L. (1990). Getting to know a good middle school: Shoreham-Wading River. *Phi Delta Kappan, 71,* 505–512.

Marks, H. M. (2000). Student engagement in instructional activity: Patterns in the elementary, middle, and high school years. *American Education Research Journal, 37,* 153–184.

Martin, W. (1988). *Control theory: Applications to middle-level school environments.* Paper presented at the Annual Meeting of the American Educational Research Association, New Orleans, LA.

Maslow, A. (1954). *Motivation and personality.* New York: Harper.

McLean, S. V., & Mayer, J. E. (1996). Social studies as child's play: Social development in early childhood. *Social Studies and the Young Learner, 9*(1), 27–29.

Metz, M. H. (1986). *Different by design: The context and character of three magnet schools.* New York: Routledge & Kegan Paul.

National Middle School Association. (1995). *This we believe: Developmentally responsive middle schools.* Columbus, OH: Author.

National Middle School Association. (2003). *This we believe: Successful schools for young adolescents.* Westerville, OH: Author.

National Reading Panel. (2000). *Teaching children to read: An evidence-based assessment of the scientific research literature on reading and its implications for reading instruction: Reports of the subgroups.* Washington, DC: National Institutes of Child Health and Human Development.

Nicholls, J. G., & Hazzard, S. P. (1993). *Education as adventure: Lessons from the second grade.* New York: Teachers College Press.

Noddings, N. (1992). *The challenge to care in schools: An alternative approach to education.* New York: Teachers College Press.

Olson, L. (1995, April 26). School portraits. *Education Week,* pp. 29–30.

Palmer, B. M., Codling, R. M., & Gambrell, L. B. (1994). In their own words: What elementary students have to say about motivation to read. *The Reading Teacher, 48,* 176–178.

Palmer, P. J. (1998). *The courage to teach: Exploring the inner landscape of a teacher's life.* San Francisco: Jossey-Bass.

Pascarella, E. T., & Pflaum, S. W. (1980). The interaction of children's attributions and level of control over error correction in reading instruction. *Journal of Educational Psychology, 73,* 533–540.

Passaro, P. D. et al. (1994). Instructional strategies for reclaiming schools. *Journal of Emotional and Behavioral Problems, 3*(1), 31–34.

Perry, C. (1998, October 14–17). *Community service learning: Goals and outcomes.* Paper presented at the annual meeting of the National Rural Education Association, Buffalo, NY.

Pflaum, S., & Bishop, P. (2004). Student perceptions of reading engagement: Learning from the learners. *Journal of Adolescent & Adult Literacy, 48,* 202–213.

Pressley, M. (2002). *Reading instruction that works: The case for balanced teaching* (2nd ed.). New York: Guilford.

Pressley, M., & Wharton-McDonald, R. (1997). Skilled comprehension and its development through instruction. *School Psychology Review, 26,* 448–466.

Reep, B. (1996). Lessons from the gang. *School Administrator, 53*(2), 26–29.

Sachar, L. (1998). *Holes.* New York: Farrar Straus Giroux.

Schine, J. (1997). School-based service: Reconnecting schools, communities, and youth at the margin. *Theory Into Practice, 36*(3), 170–175.

Schoenlein, J. (2001). Making a huge school feel smaller. *Educational Leadership, 58*(6), 28–30.

Schubert, W. H., & Ayers, W. C. (1992). *Teacher lore: Learning from our own experience.* New York: Longman.

Shultz, J., & Cook-Sather, A. (Eds.). (2001). *In our own words: Students' perspectives on school.* Lanham, MD: Rowan & Littlefield.

Sensenbaugh, R. (1993). *Writing across the curriculum: Toward the year 2000* (ERIC Document Reproduction Service No. ED354549). Available at http://www.ericdigests.org/1993/2000.htm

Sherer, M. (2002). Do students care about learning? A conversation with Mihaly Csikszentmihalyi. *Educational Leadership, 60*(1), 12–17.

Simmons, J., & Carroll, P. S. (2003). Today's middle grades: Different structures, students, and classrooms. In J. Flood, D. Lapp, J. R. Squire, & J. M. Jensen (Eds.), *Handbook of research on teaching the English language arts* (2nd ed.). Mahwah, NJ: Lawrence Erlbaum Associates.

Slavin, R. (1994). *A practical guide to cooperative learning.* Boston: Allyn & Bacon.

Smith, C. (2000). *Writing instruction: Current practices in the classroom* (ERIC Document Reproduction Service No. ED446338). Available at http://www .ericdigests.org/2001-3/writing.htm

Snow, C. E., & Others. (2002). *Reading for understanding: Toward an R&D program in reading comprehension.* Santa Monica, CA: Rand Corporation.

Soder, R. (2001). Education for democracy: The foundation for democratic character. In R. Soder, J. I. Goodlad, & T. J. McMannon (Eds.), *Developing democratic character in the young.* San Francisco: Jossey-Bass.

Soo Hoo, S. (1993). Students as partners in research and restructuring schools. *Educational Forum, 57,* 386–393.

Stevenson, C. (2002). *Teaching ten to fourteen year olds* (3rd ed.). Boston: Allyn & Bacon.

Stieglitz, E. L. (2002). *The Stieglitz informal reading inventory* (3rd ed.). Boston: Allyn & Bacon.

Stodolsky, S. S., Salk, S., & Glaessner, B. (1991). Student views about learning math and social studies. *American Education Research Journal, 28,* 89–116.

Thornton, H. (2002). A student perspective on young adolescent violence. *Middle School Journal, 34*(1), 36–42.

Tomlinson, C. (1999). *The differentiated classroom: Responding to the needs of all learners.* Alexandria, VA: Association for Supervision and Curriculum Development.

Tomlinson, C. (2001). *How to differentiate instruction in mixed-ability classrooms.* Alexandria, VA: Association for Supervision and Curriculum Development.

Turner, J. C., Meyer, D. K., Anderman, E. M., Midgley, C., Gheen, M., Kang, Y., & Patrick, H. (2002). The classroom environment and students' reports of avoidance strategies in mathematics: A multimethod study. *Journal of Educational Psychology, 94,* 88–106.

U.S. Department of Education. (2001). *What democracy means to ninth-graders: US Results from the international IEA civic education study.* National Center for Education Statistics. Washington, DC: U.S. Government Printing Office.

Van Bockern, S. (1998). Meeting the needs of our youth. *Reclaiming Children and Youth: Journal of Emotional and Behavioral Problems, 7*(3), 172–175.

Van Hoose, J., Strahan, D., & L'Esperance, M. (2001). *Promoting harmony: Young adolescent development and school practices.* Westerville, OH: National Middle School Association.

Vygotsky, L. (1978). *Mind in society: The development of higher psychological processes.* Cambridge, MA: Harvard University Press.

Wasley, P. (2000). *Small schools, great strides.* New York: Bank Street College of Education.

Wasley, P. A., & Lear, R. J. (2001). Small schools, real gains. *Educational Leadership, 58*(6), 22–27.

Weber, S. (n.d.). *Analysing visual qualitative data.* Available at http://www.iirc.mcgill .ca/methodology/about.html

Weber, S., & Mitchell, C. (1995). *That's funny, you don't look like a teacher: Interrogating images and identity in popular culture.* London: Falmer.

Wehlage, G. G., Rutter, R. A., Smith, G. A., Lesko, N., & Fernandez, R. R. (1989). *Reducing the risk: Schools as communities of support.* New York: Falmer.

Weis, M., & Hickman, T. (2003). *The nightmare lands.* Dragonlance Young Reader Novels. Renton, WA: Wizards of the Coast.

Wigfield, A. (2000). Facilitating children's reading motivation. In L. Baker, M. J. Dreher, & J. T. Guthrie (Eds.), *Engaging young readers: Promoting achievement and motivation.* New York: Guilford.

Wood, C. (1999). *Time to teach, time to learn.* Greenfield, MA: Northeast Foundation for Children.

Index

**CORWIN
PRESS**

The Corwin Press logo—a raven striding across an open book—represents the union of courage and learning. Corwin Press is committed to improving education for all learners by publishing books and other professional development resources for those serving the field of K–12 education. By providing practical, hands-on materials, Corwin Press continues to carry out the promise of its motto: **"Helping Educators Do Their Work Better."**